A Life That MATTERS

The Legacy of Terri Schiavo
A Lesson for Us All

By *Terri's Family* …

Mary and *Robert Schindler*
with *Suzanne* and *Bobby Schindler*

Scripture taken from the NEW AMERICAN STANDARD BIBLE©, Copyright © 1960, 1962, 1963, 1968, 1971, 1972, 1973, 1975, 1977, 1995 by The Lockman Foundation. Used by permission.

Cover Design by Nicholas DeRose
Painting of Terri Schindler Schiavo by Paula Hawkins

Printed in the United Stated of America

ISBN: 978-0-615-74275-5

To our beloved Terri,
And to all with disabilities, wounded in body or spirit,

May God always be your never-ceasing fountain
Of strength, consolation, and joy.

May you be seen as our society's greatest treasures.

Acknowledgments

With special thanks to Richard Marek, who, with patience and enthusiasm, helped us mold our painful memories into a cohesive narrative; to our agents, Joni Evans and Mel Berger; to Michael and Alexandra for their endless support and special love; to Mike and C.B. for all their help during such a difficult time; to David Gibbs, Pat Anderson, and Joe Magri, and all of the attorneys who represented us passionately and selflessly in the legal battle; to Monsignor Thaddeus Malanowski and all the clergy, who provided spiritual support when we needed it most; to the many politicians for showing great courage; to the Disability Groups and all the organizations that stood with us; and to the millions of people who supported and loved Terri as she fought for her life.

Robert S. Schindler, Sr., of Gulfport, Florida, father of the late Terri Schindler Schiavo, passed away August 29, 2009, from heart failure at Northside Hospital in St. Petersburg, Florida.

Robert fought valiantly to save the life of his brain-injured daughter, Terri, in the landmark right-to-life case that culminated in her imposed death by court-ordered starvation and thirst on March 31, 2005. After Terri's death, along with his wife, Mary, daughter Suzanne, and son Bobby Schindler, he founded the Terri Schindler Schiavo Foundation in St. Petersburg dedicated to supporting other families faced with the same need to fight for the rights of their disabled or otherwise vulnerable loved ones.

Robert was born in Philadelphia on October 23, 1937, and was 71 years of age. Preceded in death by his daughter, Theresa Schindler. He is survived by his wife, Mary, daughter Suzanne, son Bobby, and granddaughter Alexandra.

Contents

Preface

We are not the people you think we are.

You know us from television, surrounded by microphones, fighting for Terri's life, and you might easily have the misconception that we're political people, unreasonable people, even fanatics. Instead, we're an intensely private family who loathe the spotlight and would have given anything not to have it shine on us. The tragedy of our adored Terri made us public figures, symbols in a case that bitterly divided the country.

Our story is not the one we believe you were told, the one you saw on television and read in the newspapers. Our story—the real story—has never been told; no one, not even our closest friends, knew the struggles we went through mentally and emotionally as fifteen terrible years went by.

Yes, we sought what public tools we could—sometimes it was the politicians, sometimes the media, always the courts—so we could stand as advocates for a woman who couldn't defend herself. What family wouldn't? But to do so was agony, and each of us wants now to retreat into our own grief, our private prayers, our silent sorrow.

A year ago, our girl was lost to us. The outpouring of support couldn't save her; the condolence letters, cards, and notes cannot bring her back. We lost. Terri lost. America lost. In upholding Michael Schiavo's petition to have his wife's life terminated, the courts ruled for death over life, and we are individually and collectively diminished by their decision.

Many people have asked us to write a book, and we've always said no, refusing to open ourselves up to the pain of public display all over again. But we keep thinking of Terri and how she died, and we realize we owe her this book as a way of making sure that what happened will never happen again. Millions of people wrestle with the question of what they'd do if they faced our situation. This book, born of the pain of the past, may guide them to the answer. We believe that Terri was nothing less than the victim of judicial murder. And if revealing ourselves as we really are, and Terri as she really was, means that no one else shares Terri's fate, then our story will be the one memorial Terri would have wanted.

A Life That
MATTERS

Where there is love, there is no burden.

Brother Anthony Sweere, f.b.p.

March 30–31, 2005

I was not with Terri the night before she died. Neither was my husband, Bob. But Bobby, our son, and Suzanne, our daughter, were in her hospice room. They felt, rightly, that the sight of her would cause me and Bob too much pain. As always, they wanted to protect us.

Terri had been without food and water for thirteen days. Every motion, petition, and appeal to reinsert her feeding tube had been denied by courts throughout Florida and by the U.S. Supreme Court itself. We were not sure when death would come. We only knew that starvation is inexorable, and since there was no hope, we prayed for her comfortable release.

Her story is unique because it involved a pope and a president, movie stars, radio personalities, and prominent politicians. There's nothing unusual, however, about the loss of a child. Such tragedies are daily events. And the moral, religious, and ethical issues surrounding Terri surround all similar tragedies. Bob and I believe that God put Terri on earth to serve as a beacon, that she was taken from us so that others who suffer Terri's plight will not be taken from those who love them. That is why we've written this book.

And we start with her death, knowing it is an inspiration.

❧

My daughter, Suzanne, begins:

"The hospice facility was about a quarter mile away from a major thoroughfare and only accessible from one intersecting narrow street. That street was lined with a temporary orange mesh fence the police erected to prevent any parking near the hospice. Huge crowds gathered behind the fence, as though they were there to watch a parade. Many were in wheelchairs, disabled, brought by loved ones so they could show their support. Some held banners urging Florida Governor Jeb Bush to intercede on Terri's behalf. Others proclaimed Terri's right to live. As you drove into the street, you came to a barricade. To go beyond, you had to show the police your identification. In time they recognized me and the members of my family, but we had to show our ID, anyway.

"Once past the barricade, we were free to go to our 'home away from home,' a little odds-and-ends shop across the street from the hospice. Its owner, Stephanie Willets, who couldn't have been more generous or more giving of herself, had cleared a space for us and brought in an area rug, a couch, end tables and lamps, a refrigerator, and a few chairs. It was like a little private room, just large enough for the four of us Schindlers, though there were friends and family who came to visit. Outside, there was an absolute zoo. If the door opened even a hair, there were about fifty cameras and media people waiting for us—*Maybe there's a family member coming out! Let's grab 'im.*

"When Bobby and I went to see Terri on the night of March 30, we called two of the several policemen who were guarding the hospice entrance, a call any of us had to make when we wanted to go to the hospice. They acted as an escort, because there was no way we could make it across the street by ourselves without getting mauled. This night—it must have been about nine o'clock—the police came over, and we made a human chain. A few bystanders actually helped clear the way to the driveway of the hospice. Father Frank Pavone was with us, part of the chain. Five foot six, in his mid-forties, with dark hair and glasses, he was mild-mannered, unassuming, calm, reasoned—and one of the most inspirational people we've ever known. He had become a dear friend to us, and we felt he was able to comfort Terri.

"The driveway was blockaded against the media, and there was a row of cops. We could have walked freely from the beginning of the driveway to the hospice, but we nevertheless had to stop. The police had set up one of those white canopy tents, and we had to go inside it so they could check our ID and radio the hospice to make sure it was clear for us to enter. K-9 police dogs beyond the tent and snipers on the rooftops overlooking the hospice acted as additional guards.

"We had to be approved to enter because Michael Schiavo, Terri's husband, could, at will, turn us back. That went for our parents as well. It was particularly hard on them. We could be kept from seeing Terri for hours and hours. There was no explanation, just 'Michael Schiavo says no.' If that was the case, we'd have to be escorted back to the shop and wait for the police to come get us when it was okay to come over.

"This night we were allowed to proceed. There was another blockade at the front door, and the police made everybody—not just us, but anyone visiting a patient at the hospice—sign in and show identification. I'm not sure if they searched other people with metal detectors, but we were carefully wanded. We had to empty out all our pockets. We had to leave our purses and wallets behind.

"Once we were cleared, we could walk down the hallway to Terri's room, where there were another two policemen outside. Again we had to sign in and show our ID. And even then, we were chaperoned by the police into Terri's room."

My son, Bobby, continues:

"I remember walking into the room, looking at Terri and, in a rage, thinking, *Look what they've done to my beautiful sister.* It's hard watching someone dear to you being killed.

"The sight of Terri was awful," Bobby continues. "Her skin was discolored, and there was blood pooling in her eyes, which were darting wildly back and forth. Her cheeks were hollowed out, and her teeth were protruding. She looked like a skeleton from a horror movie.

"She was gasping for air. Earlier when I'd seen her, she was moving spastically, like she was in extreme pain and suffering. This night she lay almost still, but you could see she was scared and in pain.

"By that point, I was resigned that it was all over. I was praying that her suffering would end. It was a very intimate setting—me, Suzy, Father Frank, and Terri. I was on one side of the bed, Suzy on the other, and Father was directly across from me. He led us in prayer. We said the Rosary together, and we prayed with Father, and he sang to Terri, beautiful Latin songs. We were all holding Terri. I had my face buried on Terri's shoulder because I couldn't bear to look at her.

"I thought of how happy we all were growing up, of the vacations we took together, of the birthdays and holidays, the parties. I thought of the times Terri and I danced together, and of our grandparents whom we loved so much. And I worried about losing my parents because of all the stress they were experiencing, and I was frightened.

"One memory in particular leaped at me. I had just bought a motorcycle and went to show it to Terri, who immediately wanted me to take her for a ride. She jumped on the back and held me, her head buried in my shoulder, her arms around my waist holding on for dear life, not wanting to let go. I would have given anything to be back at that moment, Terri holding me, and me telling her not to worry, that I would never let her go.

"It was quiet in Terri's room. We were just holding her, just waiting. A sense of peace overcame me. I believe Christ's presence was with us that very instant, assuring us that in all of Terri's suffering, He was with her, with us in that room, and through Father's prayers, letting us know that we shouldn't worry about Terri, that she would be with Him soon.

"We stayed there a long time. I think until well after midnight. Then either the cops or some hospice officials told us we had to leave because it was time for Michael to visit.

"We had no choice but to leave. Suzy went home, exhausted, and Father Pavone and I went back to the room at the odds-and-ends store, where Father's friend, Jerry Horn, of Priests for Life, was waiting for us. The three of us sat and talked and prayed, but I was getting more and more nervous. We kept calling the guards asking if we could get back in, and they kept saying no.

"What made me so edgy was that two days earlier, an obituary of Terri was released on CBSNews.com.[1] It said that, made up and dressed, she died surrounded by stuffed animals, Michael—'her only love'—by her side. It's true that she had stuffed animals, but I don't think after what we'd seen that she could be described as dressed and made up, and it *certainly* wasn't true that she was dead! The obituary was all hearts and flowers, scripted for public consumption, so everybody would think Terri had died peacefully.

"We believed the only explanation was that Michael or his lawyer, George Felos, had imagined her death as they wished it and had given CBS the story, and that CBS had run it before Terri died. It was appalling! Now, in the middle of the night, I remembered it, and it scared me.

"I rushed over to the police, paying no attention to the people outside the hospice. 'When are we going back in?' I asked. And they said, 'We haven't heard anything yet. We'll let you know.'

"The hospice had told my parents that they would call if Terri was near dying, and Mom and Dad, emotionally spent, had gone home to wash and change clothes. But suddenly I was sure that the hospice *wouldn't* call and that Terri *was* near dying—or was already dead—and I wanted my parents to see her, if they wanted to, after she died.

"By dawn, I'd heard nothing. I got mad. I went back and got Father, and the two of us held an impromptu press conference. 'Michael's preventing our family from going inside,' I said. 'He's scripting this. Felos wants Michael to be alone with her. They don't want her family members to be there.'

---

[1]   CBS later apologized for running it.

"On Michael's orders, the hospice still barred us. I thought I'd go mad with frustration. It was about 6:00 a.m., and Suzy had come back, and we kept going over, and the police kept saying, 'You can't go in.' Suzanne finally called our lead attorney, David Gibbs, and he called Felos and raised a stink. But it wasn't until 7:30 a.m. that they let us in."

"She looked even worse," Suzanne says. "She was jaundiced, but her hands were black and blue, and you could see her veins. Her skin was so thin, like a sheath. And of course she looked much more drawn. Her eyes were still full of blood, and darting, and her breathing was heavy, heavy. Father Pavone and I were on her left side. Bobby was on her right side again, and there was a policeman in the room and another one at the doorway. Father Pavone had a watch in his hand, a stopwatch. I don't know why. The policeman made him hand it over. My sister's dying, and he's worried about a watch!"

"The policeman was hovering over us," Bobby goes on. "Just standing there with his arms folded and watching us while we prayed. It was very uncomfortable. This was terribly private, and there were these policemen standing and looking.

"Father continued his prayers, singing in Latin, and we knew the end was very close. Then all of a sudden some hospice people came in—administrators and nurses—and they looked at Terri and left, and then they came back and said, 'You have to leave now. We need to assess Terri.'

"I knew what was going on, that they didn't want us to be with Terri when she died, so I said, 'We don't want to leave. We know

Terri is close to dying. We'll stay in the room.' They said, 'No. It'll just be five minutes. Wait in the hallway, and you can come back.'

"So Father, Suzy, and I walked into the hallway, and immediately a policeman got in front of us. 'You have to leave the facility.' I remember the word he used. 'Facility.'

"That's when I was ready to lose it. I said, 'What's going on here? The nurses told us that in five minutes we'd be back inside. My sister's close to dying. We want to be in the room with her. I don't care if Michael's in the room with us. We're not leaving!'

"I was belligerent. 'You know as well as I do what they're doing. Please ask Michael to let us be in the room with Terri,' I pleaded.

"The policeman got belligerent right back. 'We'll talk about this outside,' he said. 'If you don't leave, I'm going to arrest you.' I said, 'This is bull. They're scripting her death. Michael wants to be here when she dies so he can go to the media and play the loving husband.' I asked him to find an administrator, and when he came back with one, the administrator said, 'Michael Schiavo has ordered you off the premises.' 'Okay,' I said, 'I'm going to leave. But I'm coming back in fifteen, twenty minutes.' The cop said, 'If you don't have permission, I'll arrest you.' 'Fine,' I said. 'You can arrest me, then. I'm coming back. I want to be with my sister.'"

"**We stormed across the street,**" Suzanne remembers. "But one thing struck me as peculiar. The argument—and Bobby and the policeman were loud—went on right outside Terri's door. Maybe the nurse was with Terri, but Michael was nowhere in sight. I wondered why he didn't come out. I wondered whether he was even *in* the hospice, let alone by Terri's side. It's something we'll never know.

"I called David Gibbs, who was en route to the hospice, whose battles on our behalf were inspiring. 'Terri is near death,' I told him, 'and they kicked us out.' David said he'd call Felos to see what he could do.

"Then minutes later, David walked in. 'Terri passed,' he said. I began to cry."

"Felos gave a press conference," Bobby says. **"One of the first** things the press asked him was, 'Why did you throw the family out of the room before Terri died?' And Felos says, 'Because Bobby Schindler started a disturbance inside the room and had to be forcibly taken out.' It wasn't true: I'd been *outside* the room. I had made a fuss *because* they kicked us out!

"Then Felos starts describing Terri's death—Michael supposedly at her side, cradling her with stuffed animals. 'It was a peaceful, beautiful time,' he said, mimicking the CBS obituary issued two days earlier. Father Pavone, who was furious, gave his own press conference, contradicting everything Felos said.

"And Suzy called Mom and Dad to tell them Terri had died."

That was the end. The beginning was fifteen years earlier.

Chapter 1

The Collapse

*T*he phone call woke us. I watched my husband, Bob, stumble to the living room of our small condo, a matter of fifteen steps, where he picked up the receiver. It was around 5:30 a.m., February 25, 1990. Calls at that hour could only mean bad news.

"Dad, it's Michael," the voice on the other end of the line said. "There's trouble. Terri's passed out. She's unconscious. I can't wake her up."

"Call 911," Bob shouted, and slammed down the phone.[1]

"There's a problem with Terri," he said, coming back to the bedroom. We decided to call our son, Bobby, right away. Bobby, aged twenty-five, lived in the same apartment complex as Terri and Michael, whose address was 12001 4th Street North. Bob went back to the phone. "Something's happened to Terri," he whispered to Bobby, barely able to get out the words. "Michael called and said he can't wake her up. You ought to get over there right away. Check it out and call me back."

Numb, too shocked to feel pain, Bob returned to the bedroom. He has always had high blood pressure, and I was watching him with anxious eyes, close to panic over him and over Terri, yet half sure that nothing really bad had happened to our daughter. We

---

[1]   Michael Schiavo claims that he called 911 before calling Bob. We know otherwise.

had just had dinner with her that evening. Had gone to Mass with her that afternoon. None of us realized how ominous the news was. There was nothing for us to do for the moment except get dressed and wait for Bobby's report.

Over the years, Bobby never told us fully what happened when he entered Terri and Michael's apartment. The memories were too vivid, his pain too great. But now, in tears, courageous, he told the story:

"The apartment was only two hundred yards away, but I figured it would be faster by car. So I threw on some jeans and a T-shirt, drove over, got out, and went to the third floor. Michael answered the door. I went in. Terri was lying face down in the corridor between the bathroom and the living room.

"I remember it like it was only hours ago. Her torso was on top of her arms with her hands up by her neck. I could see half the side of her face, and she was having trouble breathing, like almost a gurgling sound. I leaned down and shook her shoulders and said, 'Terri, get up. Get up.' There was no response. And it was at that moment that the paramedics knocked on the door.

"Michael let them in, and actually I think he was behind me when I shook Terri's shoulder—or to my side. At first, I wasn't overly concerned. I'd seen Terri just a few hours earlier in my apartment. She was perfectly fine. I asked her to go out with me and my roommate, Craig Hicken, that night, and she said she didn't want to because she had been fighting with Michael earlier that day and she was going to wait for him to come home. So I said okay, and I remember she ironed my pants.

"So I wasn't really concerned. I thought she had just passed out. But when the paramedics got there—as soon as they went down and assessed her condition ... I mean, I knew it was serious. That's when I became frantic.

"They didn't say much. The only thing I remember, they wanted to know if there were drugs. They were really hitting us hard about drugs. *'Does your wife do drugs?' 'Does your sister do drugs?'* In fact, one of the paramedics got in my face and said, 'Look, if you don't tell us that she was doing drugs, you know we're going to hold you responsible.' I think they even threatened criminal charges against me. And I knew my sister. I never knew Terri ever doing drugs. I mean, she would drink—socially drink when we went out. But never drugs. And I was adamant. 'No. She doesn't do drugs.'

"I remember the paramedics being young. I remember them hitting Terri with the defibrillators a number of times. I remember I called my dad. I went into the living room and called my dad. And didn't know what to tell him, except that she would be taken to Humana Northside Hospital. I said it was serious, but they didn't know what was wrong with her. My dad kept asking me over and over again, 'What do you think is wrong?' And I didn't know. I didn't know what was wrong. And we just waited. And they were working on her for upwards of a half hour.

"In that time frame, the police arrived, and firemen, and more paramedics. They finally got Terri stabilized enough to put her on a bed, one of those rolling beds. I remember them taking Terri out, and I remember looking at the floor. I couldn't believe all the stuff that was on the floor—trash that they were using. You know, something they injected her with, stuff they were using on her. There was just trash everywhere. Needles everywhere. So I knew there was something seriously wrong, terribly wrong, because they were injecting her with things, I guess to try to get her heart started.

"I walked downstairs. Someone was left behind—I don't know if it was a paramedic or policeman or firefighter. I said to him, 'What's going on? What's wrong with my sister?' And I remember him saying, 'If she makes it to the hospital alive, it'll be a miracle.'

"Michael got in the ambulance with Terri. I said, 'Michael, I'll be there shortly.'

"I was hysterical. I drove home, hands shaking. I called my girlfriend at the time, Julie White, to come and get me—I could barely drive, I told her. I walked in the door of my apartment and I fell to my knees and I just started crying. I woke Craig up. He was half asleep, didn't know what was going on. I told him what had happened, and Julie got there a short time after, and then we drove to the hospital."

Chapter 2

The Hospital

*W*hen Bobby called, he hadn't told us how serious Terri's condition was. He simply said that they were taking her to Humana, and we were left to guess the rest. Our guesses were grim.

Bob and I had just seen her a few hours before. She was fine. We had dinner with her. She got in her car. She went home. We couldn't imagine what could be wrong with her. I felt confused and frightened. It seemed unreal. *This can't be happening*, I thought.

Bob's memory of that morning is strong. "We drove to the hospital. The hospital is probably a twenty-minute drive from where we live, but it felt like ten hours. It was getting light outside. But on the way up, I vividly remember seeing lights in a would-be shopping center that were brighter than the other lights. And it was strange to me that they stood out with all the night city lights or streetlights; that this cluster of lights was more illuminated."

When we got to the hospital, we went to the emergency room and asked about Terri. Nobody answered. Someone—a nurse or orderly—ushered us into a waiting room, and then a doctor came in. Dr. Samir Shah. He couldn't tell us much, only that Terri was fighting for her life. Bobby arrived, shouting, "Is she dead? Is she dead?" and I said, "No. Settle down."

But of course none of us could settle down. The words, "She's fighting for her life" had blown us away. Bobby told us that they had to use "paddles" on Terri, and he may have said something about the paramedics and police. It was hard to listen. The words didn't penetrate. I don't remember whether Michael was with us—he may have been with Terri—but all we could do was wait. Dr. Shah told us that Terri had been taken from the ER to the intensive-care unit and that until they knew more about her condition, we wouldn't be allowed to see her. Imagine! Not allowed to see our daughter.

Dr. Shah left; we were alone in the waiting room; we had no information. In the years to come, we would have many frustrations with hospitals and their staffs, but this was the worst—and it was nobody's fault. Nobody had any information. Nobody knew what was going to happen to Terri.

Around eight in the morning, I called Suzanne, who was at the University of Central Florida, and told her to come to Humana Northside. I didn't want to go into details for fear Suzanne would drive like a maniac to get there, and UCF was about two hours away. "Please just take your time," I pleaded. "Terri's alive. She's okay." (Of course, as I suspected she would, Suzanne sped to the hospital, making the drive in an hour and a half.) Both Bob and I felt the same way: we were anxious for her to get there, but we dreaded telling her about her sister's condition.

Many hours later, we were allowed to see Terri in the ICU. The sight was wrenching, almost unbearable. She was on a respirator. She had an IV in her arm. She had a tube coming out of her shoulder—it was for her heart. She had something going in her nose. She had tubes in her mouth. Her skin was ashen, her eyes were closed. To Bob, it was almost inconceivable that his daughter would live. But I had faith. *She'll be all right. She'll get through this. My daughter will not be taken away.*

Bobby didn't want to go in at all. "I didn't want to see her until I knew for sure she was going to live," he told us. "And we didn't know. That's why I was scared to see her."

Suzanne, whose arrival provided a bit of solace, was in shock. "I couldn't imagine what had happened to Terri," she says. "She was fine last I'd heard. But when I got to the hospital, I was in a panic, scared to death. Especially seeing my family's faces and the fear in their eyes."

Then came the frustrating wait for a doctor to bring us news. Every time we'd hear "Code Blue, Code Blue" over the loudspeaker, we'd all jump out of our seats and rush to the ICU, jamming together in the doorway like the Four Stooges, to be told that Terri was all right, that it was a different patient in trouble. But the shock of those announcements was nightmarish; I still cringe when there's an announcement of any kind over a public address system.

Throughout the morning and the next few days, people came to keep us company and to lend support. Michael's parents lived in Pennsylvania and came down as soon as they could, along with one of his brothers. Otherwise, the visitors were all friends of ours or members of our extended family. I called Muriel Wextrom, Terri's friend at Prudential, and all Terri's friends from work came in a steady stream: Jackie Rhodes, who was Terri's best friend, and Leuretha Gibbons, her supervisor, and Fran and Sherry and Judy and Roger. Chris Adams, Bob's second cousin, came every day, even though he and Bob had met only once or twice previously. Chris's mother had died suddenly, and Terri's misfortune hit him in the heart. He was a driver for Roadway who'd go home, get up, go to work, and come back to the hospital. All of a sudden, he was family, and true to the unspoken code of the family: every time there was a crisis, every relative would offer support.

Bob's niece, Kathy Brown, came down from Pennsylvania. Her father and Bob's brother, Fred Schindler, had been in a coma after a car accident several years earlier and, contrary to his doctor's negative prognosis, had progressed remarkably after undergoing months of rehabilitation, to the point where he was able to live on his own. Kathy was a nurse and had a lot of knowledge from working with patients in Terri's condition. "Don't listen to what the doctors say, because they're going to paint the worst scenario possible," she said. "There is a good chance, if she makes it through these early days, we can get her better. We can give her rehabilitation and we can get her better." Terri's doctors were in fact somber and discouraging, doubtful that Terri would ever come out of her coma, but Kathy's words gave us hope, and we clung to them.

At one point, Bob and Suzanne went together to the hospital chapel. They knelt in prayer. Bob told his younger daughter, "Don't worry. Everything's going to be okay. If she can just hang on and get through the crisis, everything's going to be fine, we'll get her fixed." And he believed it. After all, he'd seen his brother's recovery.

We went home to change after the second day, then returned to the hospital. Bob stayed through the first week, at one time finding himself in the hospital morgue at 3:00 a.m., having lost his way in a search for a cup of coffee—"eerie and creepy," he described it. I stayed through the second week. I slept in the waiting area on chairs that were pushed together to make beds. Bobby went back to work but came every night. After a few days, we tried to persuade Suzanne to go back to school, promising to call her if there was any change in Terri's condition. But she stayed for at least a week, until Terri was out of immediate danger.

Before Suzanne left, there *was* a change—for the worse. Terri developed a staph infection and had to be put in isolation. Now only her immediate family—the four of us and Michael and his mom and dad—were allowed to see her, and we'd have to put on robes and masks before we went in. This crisis passed, but it was only after two weeks that the doctors told us they were pretty sure that Terri would live—in what state, they could not say.

Elation mixed with sadness. We had our girl with us, and if by nothing else than force of will, we would get her better. Perhaps for the first time since Terri collapsed, we allowed ourselves to remember her as she had been.

Chapter 3

Terri

*T*erri was enchanting—warm and mischievous. She loved her family, both immediate and extended, and her close friends, and she was loved in return. Bob's mother Catherine Schindler adored Terri, showering her with affection, and she was particularly close to her maternal grandparents, whose home she visited over many summers. My father, Michael Tammaro, whom the kids called "Pepa," was typically Italian, kind, loving, generous to a fault. We learned never to ask him for things because he would rush to provide them. My mother, Cecilia, or "Mema," stout and stout-hearted, shared his kindness. Cooking was her specialty. Terri once said there was no better food in the world.

When Pepa passed away, Terri wept so long and so hard Bobby remembers that he fled the house. "I had to leave because she was crying so much," he told me. "She was devastated. I remember sitting on the front porch and I closed the door and I could still hear her crying. And I had to walk out to the street to get away from her crying because I couldn't—because I knew, you see, how she felt."

When the family dog, Bucky, died in Terri's arms it was almost as terrible. (She had once given him mouth-to-mouth resuscitation.) Her heart was pure and her selflessness legendary. Everyone else came first, whether from sharing food at the dinner table, doing chores, or caring for her beloved grandmother, her Mema, after Pepa died. Terri visited her countless times at the nursing home in

St. Petersburg where we'd brought her when Mema was unable to live on her own.

Terri used to visit her five, six days a week. And she'd get on Bobby all the time about going more. I had done volunteer work at the nursing home when my mother was there in order to be with her. It made me sad to see her so unhappy, but if Terri shared my feelings, she never complained about going.

Bobby remembers: "Telling Mema about Terri's collapse was the hardest thing we ever had to do. She was having health problems and her mind wasn't clear, so I don't know if she understood everything we said, but she cried and cried."

I remember how beautiful Terri was as a baby. Wherever we would go, strangers would stop to look at her, complimenting us on her beauty.

Maybe Terri was so dear because her start in life was tough.

She was a colicky baby; it seemed she was always throwing up. She was a terrible sleeper, waking fretful and screaming. I think of how frightened I was, even when Terri only had a slight fever and her face would get beet red. She was my first baby and I didn't know what was wrong. I'd call Bob's mom and go through the litany of symptoms. She would always try to put my mind at ease, but nevertheless, I'd be at the pediatrician's office as soon as the doors opened.

Neither Bob nor I remember getting any sleep for three months after she was born. It got so bad we sent an SOS to my mother, who came and babysat for a weekend while we disappeared to a motel just so we could get some sleep. Then, just when we finally got her settled down, along came Bobby, whose cries woke Terri up, and our sleep deprivation started all over again.

One eye used to roll to the center, giving Terri a clownish look, and only at age two, when we got her glasses, did her gaze become normal. One of her eyes wouldn't tear, and a doctor recommended surgery, but another said, "All you have to do is massage the eye and eventually it'll open up." We massaged it and put warm compresses on it, and finally her tear duct opened and she was fine.

Bobby was born thirteen months after Terri. As soon as he could crawl, Terri crawled after him like an obedient puppy, though she was able to walk by the time she was fifteen months old. She adored him from the start and followed him everywhere. Once, when she was two, our friend Jimmy brought his son over, and Bobby wanted one of his toys. The boy wouldn't give it to him, so Terri grabbed the toy and gave it to Bobby. They were like that in their adult lives, too, each fighting for the other.

Terri moved at her own pace. Unlike our other kids, she was very hard to toilet train. As far as she was concerned, she could have worn the same soiled diaper for the rest of her life. Even her teeth were slow in coming, and her second set came in crooked. A first-rate orthodontist straightened them with braces, which she wore throughout her early adolescence, and when the braces came off, her smile could have been used in a toothpaste ad. She took good care of her teeth from that point on, which made it all the sadder when, in hospice, they began decaying in her mouth.

Bob was working for Day & Zimmerman, a firm of consulting engineers. (He was soon assigned to work with the Corning glass company in Corning, New York, which was where he met me.) His job required frequent moves, and Terri was born in Philadelphia, Pennsylvania, in December 1963. When Bob's work took him to upstate New York, we lived briefly in my parents' house in Corning, then came back to a house we had bought after Terri's birth on Bloomfield Avenue in Philadelphia. That's where Bobby was born.

In 1965, Bob left Day & Zimmerman to work as a material handling salesman for his brother, Fred, who had recently started a new business. His sales career was extremely successful, so right after Suzanne was born, in June 1968, we moved again, this time to a four-bedroom house Bob had built in Montgomery County in suburban Philadelphia. The name Schindler generated considerable respect in the area.

It was awfully nice there, but its Catholic school didn't have a kindergarten, so for two years each, we enrolled the kids in public school, where I did volunteer work to be close to them. Most of our neighbors were Jewish, and we quickly became popular because we were the family with the Christmas tree and invited all the kids to watch the holiday TV specials, like Terri's favorites, *The Little Drummer Boy* and *Rudolph the Red-Nosed Reindeer*, a practice I started when the children were young and continued for seven or eight years. My children lived for those holidays, whether they involved going to Pepa and Mema's house in Corning for Thanksgiving or were celebrated at home. Terri loved them. They meant presents, cookies, visits from uncles, aunts, and cousins, and staying up later than usual. Bobby and Suzanne remember the excitement of the days, their "specialness." Not many people we speak to have such great memories of childhood; in that sense, our family was extraordinary.

After Terri collapsed, Christmas (and her birthday) were celebrated in Terri's nursing or hospice room, and I would bring decorations and cards, but poignancy replaced joy, and our gaiety was for Terri's benefit, not so much for ours.

While Terri was a generally passive child, she could fight her own battles and, if attacked, retaliate.

One of my most vivid memories was the day Bobby, aged three, locked Terri, aged four, in the large white suitcase we used when we went on trips. I found her, of course—her screams were fire-engine piercing. The blood vessels had broken in her face with the effort, and she was appropriately fire-engine red, but she calmed quickly after she was rescued and went to her room to recover. Two days later, Bobby was standing at the top of the stairs, and all of a sudden Terri was behind him, pushing him as hard as she could. He went flying down the stairs. I raced to Bobby, then, seeing he was unharmed (the stairs had been newly carpeted, which probably prevented serious injury), went up to Terri's room. Our daughter had hidden behind her bureau, but she emerged when I came in.

"I'm not going to punish you or anything," I said, "because you know what you did was wrong."

Terri was bawling. "Is he hurt? Is he hurt?" she kept repeating. "Please go down to see if he's hurt."

"I think he's all right," I told her. "But that was a terrible thing for you to do."

Terri knew it. Bobby knew that what he had done was terrible, too. From that time forward, none of our children attacked each other.

Bob and the kids teased each other all the time, and Terri's laughter—everyone who knew her spoke about how *much* she laughed—replaced her tears.

Terri could get to Bobby in psychological ways, too.

"When I was a kid growing up," Bobby told us, "I was deathly afraid of tornadoes because I'd watched *The Wizard of Oz* and saw what tornadoes did. So whenever Terri wanted to get back at me, she'd start screaming, '*Auntie Em, Auntie Em. There's a storm coming.*' It drove me crazy."

Terri disliked school, and there was nothing we could do to encourage her. Bobby and Suzanne were B students, and both preferred summers to school days (they were more athletes than scholars), but Terri's antipathy showed itself in a reluctance to do homework, a reticence to talk about school activities at dinner, and a reluctance to take part in most special school events unless we forced her. She rarely appeared in pageants or plays, for example, and as for sports—well, she took part in them as rarely as possible.

Perhaps she shunned the out-of-doors because it meant danger. Once, when Bobby and Terri were at their grandparents' house in Corning, Pepa took them for an outing in the countryside (my parents' house, spacious and welcoming, was on a tree-lined street near the center of the city). They were crossing a bridge over a creek when they were attacked by a swarm of yellow jackets.

"We got stung probably a dozen times," Bobby vividly remembers. "They were just everywhere, and they were biting us. Terri was going hysterical. I was crying, because I was little at the time, but nothing like Terri. Pepa was trying to grab us and get us back to the car, and I don't think he knew what to do. We all ran back to the car. I remember we had calamine lotion, like dots, all over us, and that helped. But Terri was scared to death.

"When we were older, and Mom and Dad took us to the Jersey Shore, she was deathly afraid of the biting green flies. She hated going to the beach because of them, though she loved staying at the motel and lying on a deck chair to get a tan."

Aside from horseback riding, which she loved, the only time we can remember Terri doing anything athletic was when she started high school. Two of her girlfriends, including her best friend, Sue Kolb, persuaded her to come with them on a school skiing trip. We sent her in the school bus—she looking a bit green—and went to pick her up at her school when the bus returned. The kids streamed out; no Terri. Finally our daughter emerged, looking like a stiff board walking. She couldn't bend her knees, didn't move her arms. All she did was clump down the stairs, wrapped in her snowsuit.

"Mom, I can't move," she wailed.

I hugged her. "What's wrong, honey?"

"I fell. All day long I kept falling."

The next day, I took her to the doctor. "She's just sore," he said. "She should get more exercise."

Terri's solution was to never go skiing again. "We used to go outside and play with the neighborhood kids," Suzanne remembers. "Freeze tag and stick ball, ice skating and baseball. She had absolutely no interest in exercising. She did *not* like to sweat."

What she loved were animals. Each of our children had their own room. Terri's, painted her favorite color, purple, was filled with so many stuffed animals she joked she could start a zoo. Because of her, we endured hamsters, guinea pigs, gerbils, rabbits, fish. Terri had her own fish tank. One of the neighborhood kids, Bret Lader, poured all the fish food in it at once and the fish died. Terri, by this time in her early teens, wanted to scream.

The death of our Labrador, Bucky, was probably the biggest trauma of Terri's early years. The love of animals never left her. When she was a teenager, she came home hysterical once, thinking she had run over a stray cat and killed it. Bob and a friend of his went to look for it, found it dead, and buried it. They told Terri it had run off chasing another cat. Only then did her tears cease. Bob claims it was the best fib he and his friend ever told.

She loved television, too, especially cartoons and, later, *Starsky and Hutch*. Bob remembers coming into her room one time to find her crying her eyes out because Lassie had been injured.

"Terri, it's not real," he said. "The dog didn't get hurt. There are people standing there with cameras. The dog's *acting*."

His reassurance did little good. A few days later he came in again to find her crying—this time over a cartoon.

We worried that she watched too many shows, that she didn't get enough fresh air. Corning was the solution. She was happy when she was with her grandparents and also when we vacationed at the Jersey Shore. She'd go to the beach, though only after we convinced her that there were no green flies, but she wouldn't go swimming. *Jaws* was the reason. She went to see it with her brother, but made him leave halfway through.

"Our routine at the shore was to pull up to our favorite motel," Bob remembers. "The kids would run out of the car and go up to the room, and I got stuck with the luggage. One summer, when she was thirteen or fourteen, I went outside and saw Terri in her nearly transparent bathing suit, stretching like a beauty pageant queen on the diving board at the pool. *She's grown*, I thought, with a mixture of awe and shock at her naïveté. I made her go inside and change her suit to something more decent."

Terri's clothes were usually jeans and a T-shirt. Her music was Loverboy, Duran Duran, and George Michael of Wham! When she wasn't at school, she stayed in her room, with the door closed, playing with her animals. Sue Kolb often came over, and I remember the sound of their giggling about boys and whatever secrets schoolgirls share. You could say she had an active fantasy life, though she wasn't particularly introverted, and maybe, as a child, was a little afraid of the real world. She spooked easily, Bob remembers. But more, he remembers her endearing laughter.

Terri began to draw when she got to junior high. Almost all her pictures were of animals—dogs and horses mostly—and we thought they were terrific. None of the rest of us had any artistic talent whatsoever, and we were awed by this aspect of her. It showed us a side of her that touched us all.

The Kolbs twice took her to Disney world, once when she was fourteen, then again at seventeen, and she fell in love with it. We had taken her earlier, but these trips with the Kolbs seemed to make a bigger impression on her. She asked us for a Mickey Mouse phone, and she drew all the Disney characters with remarkable skill. We have her drawings, of course. They are a way we remain in contact with her.

She used to kid us about wanting to work at Disney World but then, after she'd seen Joan Embrey on television, decided to become a veterinarian at the San Diego Zoo. We told her that to become a certified veterinarian she'd need a college degree— Bob was pushing her in that direction, anyway. She wrote to Ms. Embrey and received an answer. "You were right," she admitted to her father. "Joan Embrey told me I'm never going to be able to work at the zoo unless I go to college." To Suzanne, she revealed that she'd become a veterinarian assistant because she didn't want to go through all that school.

Terri was a chunky child, not a fat one. But when at age twelve she returned from a month spent with her grandparents in Corning, it looked like she had swallowed a watermelon. Her Mema, overweight herself, was a great cook and thought nothing of stuffing Terri without caring about the calories. And when Terri went to high school, for some reason she just kept gaining every year, eventually reaching upwards of two hundred pounds (she was five foot five), to the point where we worried about it. She never mentioned it herself, but I remember shopping with her, and her tearful refusal to buy the prettiest dress she picked out because she thought she looked so ugly in it. With the exception of Sue Kolb, her other friends were overweight, too, reinforcing each other and keeping her and them out of the mainstream social life of their high school class.

Suzanne, who always looked up to her, tells us she often wanted to go into Terri's room to see what she and her friends were doing. "Sometimes she was kind enough to let me in. But a lot of the times she kept the door shut and wouldn't let me enter. I never resented it. More often than not, Bobby and Terri had more of a connection because they were thirteen months apart, and I was viewed as the spoiled little sibling—the baby. So I was teased a lot. I was very different than Terri. I was more outgoing, I was more athletic. I was always doing stuff, and she really was the homebody. Terri was about five years older than me, and she really confided more in her girlfriends than she did in me. After she was married, though, I would hear about Michael."

We were concerned that Terri didn't date and refused to go to any of the proms, but she seemed happy. (Indeed, she was capable— rarely—of spontaneous gaiety. Bob remembers how it "knocked his socks off" when, at a Tony Orlando and Dawn concert, she rushed onstage when Tony Orlando asked for volunteers from the audience.)

I took her to Dr. Ickler, her pediatrician, to ask for advice about her weight. He examined Terri, then looked her in the eyes. "When you're ready to lose weight, you'll know it. Then we'll talk." He turned to me. "Now, Mom, I don't want you to bug her. I don't want you to push her or say anything about it because when Terri's ready to lose weight, she'll tell you."

The moment she graduated from high school, she came to me. "I'm ready to lose weight," she said.

I took her back to Dr. Ickler. He put her on a Nutra-System diet, at that time a new kind of weight-loss regimen, and slowly, gradually, the pounds came off.

Her loss of weight triggered a transformation in Terri that thrilled us and delighted her friends. From a stay-at-home, she became a girl who loved to socialize. Her sense of humor, until then sly and quiet, blossomed. She could be the loudest in a group, the least inhibited, given to teasing and being teased. By the time she was twenty, she had lost forty pounds. Friends and strangers commented on the beauty of her figure. She became sure of herself, unafraid to voice her opinions, the center of attention rather than at its outskirts. And her laughter! It seemed to me everything struck her funny, and her glee was evident, her joy of being alive.

It was not surprising that this vibrant, graceful, blossoming girl would attract men. Nor, in retrospect, was it surprising that Terri, sexually innocent and naïvely unaware of the effect of her new power on others and on herself, would fall hard for the first attractive man who fell for her.

She did. His name was Michael Schiavo.

Chapter 4

Terri and Michael

*T*erri was in love. Blond, blue-eyed, six-foot-six Michael Schiavo, at twenty-one, a year older than Terri, was the first boy she had ever dated, and she thought being out with him was romantic and grown-up. They had met in 1982 in a sociology class at Bucks County Community College in Pennsylvania, and when he asked her out for the first time, she was so excited she asked a friend to come down from college and help her with her clothes and makeup.

On their second date, he brought her a single red rose and shortly afterward asked her to marry him.

As a younger teenager, she had fantasized about marriage, often stopping in front of bridal shops and imagining herself in the wedding dresses. It's hard to know what she fantasized about Michael, but in retrospect, I believe it was the man of her dreams she wanted to marry, not the person she eventually wed.

As we got to know Michael, we began to refer to him as "Mr. Charm." He was almost always polite, but his words and behavior toward us seemed rehearsed, as though he was holding something in, something he didn't want us to see. Michael's parents were blue-collar, Lutheran, rock-solid. Michael was the last of five boys, and I was happy when I met his parents, for they struck me as gentle and kind. It was easier for our family to maintain a friendship with them, in fact, than it was with Michael. Bob in particular was uncomfortable around him. "He doesn't seem real," he'd complain. We didn't know which Michael would show up on any given day.

The important thing, though, was that Terri was happy. Michael introduced her to a kind of life she had never known. They went frequently to bars and neighborhood restaurants, where Terry enjoyed the social drinking and the flattery of not only Michael but of other young men who obviously found her as attractive as he did. Terri dropped out of college and got a job as a field-service representative for Prudential Insurance. Just before their marriage, Michael was employed at a McDonald's, one of a string of restaurant jobs that he had throughout their relationship.

When Terri told us they were planning to get married, I was horrified, as I probably would have been no matter her choice. She was still a girl, an inexperienced, naïve girl, I felt, and Bob and I tried to talk her out of it. But she was so obviously in love that our hearts softened, and soon we kept our objections to ourselves.

They dated for one year, Terri more and more sure she was making the right choice. Her certainty eased our fears. We offered her a choice of a gift of $10,000 or a $10,000 wedding.

"The wedding!" Terri exclaimed. "It's what I've always wanted."

Terri never looked more beautiful.

She wore a white wedding dress with lace sleeves and a choker collar, a large hat adorned with lace, and a hundred-megawat smile. The wedding was fun, a party. It was a Catholic ceremony (Michael was given special dispensation), held at our local parish, and afterward there was a reception for more than two hundred people at a restaurant called Hampton Inn. Suzanne, sixteen, Terri's maid of honor, remembers thinking, *Wow, this is cool!* I thought so, too. For a honeymoon, they went to our condominium in Florida. My doubts about the marriage—that Terri was too young, that Michael was the wrong man for her—receded.

The newlyweds rented an apartment, but it proved too expensive for them, so they moved into our newly redecorated and furnished recreation room in the basement. We weren't particularly happy about the arrangement, and I don't think Terri and Michael were, either. We tended to pussyfoot around each other, careful not to get in the way, but we were always cordial. Terri worked days, and Michael worked nights at McDonalds.

In 1984, Bob sold his business and planned to move to Florida, which we did two years later. Terri asked if she and Michael could move to Florida with us, and they preceded us there by a few months. Terri was out of work, though she was eventually hired by Prudential. Michael had a number of restaurant jobs. We rented a house, while they stayed in our condo, which we had owned for many years. Michael agreed to pay half the rent. After getting and giving up several jobs over the course of three years, Michael became manager at Agostino's, an Italian restaurant in St. Petersburg, and they settled into their own apartment, about a twenty-minute drive from our house.

Those were the living arrangements when Terri collapsed. But much more than a change of location was taking place within the marriage.

⧼⧽

It was Bobby who first sensed that something was wrong. "Once we moved to Florida, Terri and I became closer than ever," he told us as we tried to analyze what had gone wrong for the purposes of this book. "Michael was working nights, and Terri and I both worked during the day, so we would call each other two or three times a day, and would often go out at night. We'd go to clubs together. I was single and in my early twenties, and that was part of my life back then. She would join me and my friends, and we'd have fun. There were guys asking her to dance. She would giggle. I would laugh at her, how she would respond to it, because I thought it was hilarious she was so flattered by it. I don't think she knew how to react.

"I remember one time we were at Bennigan's. And this local sports anchor was really hitting on Terri. She was giggling and interacting with him. She had this naïveté about her, and she would talk to him, but that's all it really amounted to. She was beginning to realize that she attracted other men. Because of her self-esteem, I don't think she ever expected that to happen to her. And as a joke, she would often tell people that I was her boyfriend. She never mentioned she was married.

"There was nothing wrong with what she was doing. She never went home with any of the guys—she was just flirting. She was as devout as any twenty-two-year-old woman could be. I mean, she went to church every Sunday. I *know* she was receiving the sacraments.

"I sensed that she would rather be with her family than she would with Michael. She was able to be her true self when she was away from him."

Michael and Bobby never got along. "We tolerated each other," Bobby said, "but we were not close at all. I felt like I always had to try my hardest not to inflame the relationship. We always seemed as though we were on the verge of a confrontation. And one time when Terri and Michael were dating, we got into it in the living room. I don't remember what the fight was about. But Terri was there, and my ex-girlfriend was there, Cindy. I remember Terri and Cindy saying, 'Stop! Settle down.' But he didn't stop. I said something that must have hit a nerve, and he went crazy. He pushed me down on the couch and had me with his hand around my throat. I couldn't move. And he had his fist cupped in the air. He was ready to punch me. Terri and Cindy were frantic. 'Stop. Stop!' And he did. He let me go. He outweighed me probably by seventy, eighty pounds. And he scared me. From then on, I was scared of him ever reaching that point again. I remember Terri begging me not to say anything about it to anybody. That was the only violent episode I had, but I knew there were others with other people, such as the one with Suzanne."

Suzanne described it. "Actually there were two times. When they were first married, I spent a lot of time with Terri and Michael. There were often times when Michael was roughhousing with both of us. He would pinch. He used to grab the back of your arm and he would twist. Here today I cringe because it hurt really bad. I would see bruises on Terri, and she would always brush them off as horseplay, but I would get angry and he and I would fight because the horseplay got real physical. And he did not like me. I mean, he wasn't going to control me. Terri was definitely more passive. If she would stand up to him in front of other people, I'm sure she heard about it when we all left, behind closed doors.

"The other time was really scary. We were all living in a rented house in Vina del Mar when Terri was well enough to be moved from the hospital to live with us. It was in '91, right before I got married, so I was living at the house, and I had the same kind of situation Bobby described. I had to keep my mouth shut a lot, just to forestall any arguments. I don't remember exactly why we fought, but I'll bet it was about how disrespectful he was to all of us, and how he was too moody. And everyone was so good to him at that time, that's what bothered me. We treated him like a son or a brother.

"I must have opened my mouth to him. I mean, he was rude! Terri was in her room, in her wheelchair, and I was grateful she couldn't hear us. It really bugged me how he had no respect and he was not a kind person. I had said something, and I remember he just went from zero to sixty, and then he started to come after me. And I think dad stepped between us."

Bob remembers the fight clearly. "He came across the room after her, and I jumped in between the two of them. I thought he was going to hurt her. He backed off. I said to Suzanne, 'When you go in your bedroom tonight, lock the door.' I didn't know what Michael was going to do.

"Michael was under a psychiatrist's care at the time, and I got so upset I called the psychiatrist in Bradenton and described the incident with Suzanne. And he said to me, 'If it ever happens again, call the police immediately.' That scared the hell out of me because we were all living in the same household. 'Keep a hammer under your pillow,' I told Suzanne. 'Just in case.'"

Suzanne and Michael didn't speak after that. A month later, she was married and out of the house. But I was left to think of the implications of Bob's advice. A hammer under her pillow? Did Terri need similar protection? How many times had Michael turned his anger on her? The questions tortured me. What happened in their marriage that I didn't know about? How much had Terri kept from me?

The kids' stories reminded me of a time in Pennsylvania right after Terri and Michael married.

Our whole family was up to his parents' house. We were having a barbecue, and everybody else was outside. I was sitting at the kitchen table—I don't remember why—and Michael came into the kitchen with his brother Scott. All of a sudden the trash can went flying and they started hitting each other and Michael grabbed Scott around the neck and got him in a choke hold. And they were fighting and arguing, and Michael pushed Scott down, choking him. Then his father came in and they stopped fighting, but Scott was in pain. There was obviously a violent streak in "Mr. Charm" beneath his social politeness.

It seemed to us that Michael was angry most of the time. No matter what restaurant he was working at, the owners and managers who were running them "didn't know the first thing about it," he'd say. They were "stupid jerks" and "bums" who didn't let him do his job right. Neither Bob nor I can remember a time when Michael took the blame for anything, and naturally it worried us that he might be acting the same way toward Terri. Terri told Suzanne that he was angry she spent so much time with us and her siblings. He didn't like it when Terri went out with her girlfriends, either. "I think it was a control issue," Suzanne says. "Besides, they worked on opposite schedules. Why shouldn't she spend time with us when he was away?"

In the early days, Terri didn't say much to any of us about her marriage, but from time to time, she did complain to Suzanne about some of the things Michael was doing. "Like marking down the mileage on her car before he would go to work. And then verifying with her where she went when he got home to make sure it matched up with the miles on the odometer."

He monitored her expenses as well as her mileage, and was furious when she spent money on herself. Terri's best friend, Jackie Rhodes, says that on the day before she collapsed, Terri told her in a tearful phone conversation that she and Michael had quarreled bitterly because she had spent eighty dollars to color her hair blond. Michael wanted it brown because it was less expensive to maintain. Jackie was contemplating a divorce at the time, and Terri told her she was thinking about divorcing Michael. The two even went window-shopping for furniture in case they decided to share an apartment.

I wasn't surprised when I found out that Terri had wanted a divorce. It hurt, of course, because it proved how unhappy Terri must have been. She was a fighter. She'd have stayed with almost any bad situation and tried to solve it. She must have been so desperate, to go against the teaching of our religion, and I realized she was too ashamed to confide in me. The battle in her soul must have been awful.

Despite his attacks on Terri for her "extravagance," Michael spent freely on himself, especially on jewelry, even when he was out of work. Suzanne's husband, Dan, whom she subsequently divorced, was financially comfortable, and Michael looked up to him, spending as much time with him as possible, as though to partake of wealth.[1] Suzanne remembers that when Dan went to Cleveland to visit his parents, Michael would call him several times a day. "It was very odd. There were months when he'd call him incessantly. We all began to question it, and it got so bad that Dan's mother would call down here and say, 'Why is Michael calling so often? What's going on?' I think eventually Dan told him to stop because it was out of hand and it was odd. And Terri couldn't explain it."

When Terri and Michael were living with us in Philadelphia, Terri came to Bob one day. "Daddy, look at this," she said. She showed him a wristwatch, a Rolex or a Lucien Piccard. "It's magnificent," Bob said. And she said, "Well, he bought it for a co-worker." Bob was furious. "You guys don't even have enough money to rent an apartment, and he's spending that kind of money for a watch for a casual friend.

Still, Terri rarely complained, at least to us. She confided that her sex life with Michael was deteriorating. On two occasions, she told me that Michael would say he worked all night and was too tired. Once, in tears, she said Michael told her "he just didn't want it."

I was astounded. To me, his disinterest in sex meant he wasn't interested in her. It was my first inclination that something wasn't right in their marriage.

Terri's outlet was harmless flirtations, one with the UPS man who came to the Prudential office every day. Sometimes they would

---

[1]   Many of Bob's friends cautioned him that Michael might have expected a position in Bob's company after he and Terri were married.

lunch together, and she would tell her best friend at work, Jackie Rhodes, how handsome she thought he was. One day Bob picked her up for lunch at the Prudential offices. A co-worker said something to Terri about the guy, and Bob asked her about him. "Her face went red. 'Nothing, Daddy. Nothing, Daddy.' Very defensive."

"Well, she was human," Suzanne says about the incident. "The guy was nice to her. They laughed together. She told me he was funny. And they did go to lunch. Of course Michael never knew about it.

"It was all innocent. I remember we used to go to a restaurant called Crabby Bill's—a group of our friends and Mom and Dad's friends. Terri was funny because there was a bartender in there and—oh, God, he was this scary-looking guy. He had tattoos. Rough-looking but attractive. And Terri thought he was just so cute. And I think he google-eyed her too, because she'd colored her hair blond and she looked great. She was tan, I'll tell you, she was just beautiful.

"I thought it was terrific that she had dyed her hair. That she was feeling so good about herself. After all the time she spent alone when she was growing up, here she was, out of her shell, enjoying herself."

After a similar flirtation with a waiter, Bob and Terri went to a Mass at St. John's. Terri, looking angelic in a white dress, went to Communion, and afterward Bob teased, "I hope you went to Confession, too." And our sweet, good girl looked at him and said very seriously, "I don't have to because I have nothing to confess."

I knew less about the downward spiral of Terri's marriage than our children did. With Suzanne away at school, Bobby became her closest confidante. And several weeks before she collapsed, she told Bobby what she told Jackie later: that she wanted a divorce.

"We were at Bennigan's with Michael and Michael's brother Brian, who was in St. Petersburg on vacation. We were having dinner. She said, 'I have to go to the bathroom,' and she asked me to come with her. I couldn't imagine why, but of course I went with her. As we were walking to the bathroom, she stopped right in front of the door. And just broke down. Started crying. She said that her relationship was horrible. She wanted to divorce him, but felt she could never do it. She didn't have the courage or the guts. And she was a devout Catholic. She wasn't *supposed* to get divorced.

"I was shocked. I'd no idea things were that bad. Because she'd never really opened up to me like this about her relationship with Michael. I could sense there wasn't a lot of affection there the last couple of years—that there was contention between them. She'd make snide remarks about him, about his attitude and how moody he was. But still—*divorce*?

"I said, 'Did you talk to mom and dad about this?' And she was emphatic. 'No. I would never tell mom and dad. Don't you say anything to them. I don't want to upset them.' We were all very concerned about upsetting my parents, so that was it. I told her, 'If there's anything I can do to help ...' and I might have suggested she see a marriage counselor. But it threw me."

~~∽✸∽~~

If only Bobby had told me, I think now. *If only Terri had confided in me.* Would it all have turned out different? Would we have supported her to leave him? Would leaving him have saved her life?

Chapter 5

Early Days

"*Y*our daughter is PVS," Dr. Garcia DeSousa, Terri's neurologist, said, taking my hand at the side of Terri's bed, toward the end of Terri's second week at Humana Northside after her collapse.

I looked at him uncomprehendingly. "What does PVS mean?"

"Persistent vegetative state. It's a condition where the patient is, and will remain, unconscious and unaware." His tone was sympathetic. "As long as we keep feeding her, she won't die from it, but this is how it's going to be. She's never going to get any better."

News like that is impossible to digest. Bob and I took it in without processing it and without considering its implications. Our grief was so intense, our minute-by-minute advocacy for Terri so fierce, that DeSousa's diagnosis felt simply like one more piece of bad news. Besides, "persistent vegetative state" certainly *didn't* describe Terri, who had already responded to our presence with smiles, and whose eyes were able to follow our movements around the ICU.

Michael himself, in his notebook written between April and May 1990, which he showed to me at the time, notes that Terri was able to follow voices; respond to his questions by nodding; was obviously dreaming; could squeeze her nurse's hand; cried; was able to hold her head up and turn it; and could move her whole body around in the bed. As I read his words now, I get teary. He *saw* the potential for Terri's recovery. He *wanted* it. Implicitly he was ready to *fight* for it. He made a commitment to Terri and our family to help her. It was he who soon changed his mind, not Terri.

True, even at the beginning, there were times, even days, when she was unresponsive, but more often than not she was with us. And it was inconceivable to us that she wouldn't get better. Hadn't Bob's niece, Kathy Brown, a trained nurse, already warned us not to listen to the doctors, because they always gave the worst-case scenario?

We dismissed the diagnosis and, with Michael, planned for the first steps in Terri's rehabilitation. Yet it was a diagnosis that was to haunt us for fifteen years.

Within twenty-four to forty-eight hours after Terri's collapse, Dan Grieco, a lawyer who was also Michael's boss at Agostino's restaurant, approached us in the ICU waiting room. "In order to expedite Terri's medical care, it would be better if one person deals with the doctor," he said.

Grieco made sense. There would obviously be many times to come when we would not all be together when a medical decision about Terri's care was necessary. Even at the hospital, every time a doctor emerged from the ICU, there were five people—Michael and all the Schindlers—who ganged up on him, and the result was chaotic.

Michael was the logical choice, given that there was nothing written by Terri to say otherwise. He was, after all, Terri's husband;

she was his primary "responsibility." Grieco subsequently brought the documents authorizing Michael to be the liaison between the family and the medical staff at Northside, and Bob and I signed it.

We didn't realize—and our naïveté in those early days now seems to Bob and me mind-boggling, even given our extreme duress—that we had essentially given Michael power of attorney. It was a document that permitted him to intercede for us with Terri's doctors, to deal with the medical staff and *relay* information. He could filter that information as he wished. If he wanted to hide something from us, either good news or bad, we could not prevent him.[1]

None of this would have mattered if Michael and we had remained a team. For the first two years, we acted in concert, everybody working for Terri, everybody thinking first about her well-being. We didn't consider the consequences of signing those papers. The only thing on our minds was that Terri was fighting to stay alive, and we devoted all our energies to joining her in that fight.

During this time, Michael told Bobby that Grieco had mentioned the possibility of instituting a medical malpractice lawsuit. We shelved this notion in the back of our brains. Michael didn't.

---

[1] Fourteen years later, Bobby and Suzanne went to the courthouse to look for the papers and found they were not there. What they discovered instead were papers granting Michael guardianship over Terri which he had applied for and was granted in a court hearing in June 1990. Although Michael claimed otherwise, we had no idea that such a hearing was held, nor did we know its outcome. Dan Grieco was his attorney.

❧

In early April of 1990, Terri's medical condition had improved so much she was transferred from the intensive-care unit to a progressive-care unit. Almost immediately a new crisis emerged, which did not affect Terri's health but was traumatic to us nevertheless. Terri was a full-time employee of Prudential at the time of her collapse, so its health insurance arm, PruCare, covered most of her hospital bills at the beginning. By the end of April, PruCare served notice it was withdrawing her medical coverage and advised Humana Northside to begin preparations for her release.

We made sure the local media got the story. PruCare became embarrassed at the attention, and we were able to negotiate a transfer for Terri from Humana Northside to College Harbor nursing home in St. Petersburg. But it was only a momentary respite. A financial burden loomed before us, and we could only guess how large it would become.[2]

Indeed, in June 1990, Prudential terminated Terri's coverage for good and pressured College Harbor to release her to our care.[3] We would have welcomed such a move with happy hearts, but a better alternative presented itself: Dr. David Baras, the medical director of the Bayfront Medical Center's rehabilitation facility, who had examined Terri when she was at Northside, announced she had improved from her initial deep coma, and recommended she

---

[2] Bob's brother Fred's business had flourished, but after Fred's wife and daughter were killed in an automobile accident, he sold it to Bob and another employee. Bob served as president and CEO of the corporation, but in 1984 sold his stock. His income dipped even as his goal of spending more time with his family was achieved.

[3] Michael sued Prudential, but the suit was quickly thrown out of court.

begin a rehabilitation program at Bayfront, also in St. Petersburg. She moved there at our expense.

Her improvement was gradual, but we saw signs of it every day. She squeezed our hands harder. She tried to sit up on her own. We kept comparing notes with Michael: "Did you see her move?" "Terri tried to say 'Michael' and 'Mom.'" "She tried to get up from her chair." I remember my own surge of hope. My daughter would come back to me. With rehabilitation, I thought, it was possible she would walk again, talk again, once again become my Terri.

In August, Terri, had advanced enough that we were able to continue rehabilitation and therapy for her at home. We had rented a three-bedroom house in Vina del Mar so that Michael could live comfortably with us.

What joy it gave us to have her with us! To be able to hold her and kiss her in a room that smelled like home instead of a hospital, uninterrupted by nurses and loudspeakers blaring for a doctor's attention. To bathe her, to clothe her, to take her outdoors. Now there was no question of PVS. This was an injured girl, not a comatose one. Terri was responsive to everything around her. She would laugh at our jokes, smile when we sang to her. She was a *presence* in our lives, interacting with us as best she could.

She loved going to the mall. The county paid for wheelchair transport; all we had to do was put her in the chair, and they would pick us up and take us back. When she was tired, she'd start fidgeting, and her groans would tell us it was time to sleep. Through the use of a Hoyer lift, we were able to get her in and out of the hospital bed donated by one of our friends. When she lay in it, she was connected to a G-tube in her stomach through which we fed her formula, a lot like Ensure, which kept her robust; it was the only tube to which she was attached. (A feeding tube through the nose was judged too dangerous because it could so easily become infected.) The nurses at Bayfront had told us how to care for her but hadn't warned us that the G-tube would sometimes come out and have to be replaced at the hospital. Frantic calls to the EMTs were the result.

Bob worked as a mechanical systems designer for Raytheon Engineers during the day, so Michael and I divided the custodial duties. We had to be careful that Terri didn't choke on her own phlegm. Michael, who was taking nurses' training courses, insisted it was his "job" to use the suctioning device provided by Bayfront, and he became expert at it, as well as using the G-tube. Terri was up most of the day and often slept through the night, but Michael and I took turns staying with her at night just to make sure she was okay. It made us feel better, knowing she was never unattended.

Michael and I became very close during this period, treating each other as partner and friend. Michael never talked about his feelings or about his childhood, but he fought hard for his wife and was tireless in her care. A bond grew between us, which was not the case between Michael and Bob. In fact, Michael said in a deposition years later something to the effect that Bob "didn't want to participate in helping Terri," an accusation that stung because it was so obviously untrue.

Still, by October, Michael and I decided we could care for Terri no longer. There had been too many trips to the hospital to have the G-tube reinserted, too many calls to the paramedics when Terri had coughing fits we did not know how to stop. All the good will in the world couldn't substitute for the sheer physical burden placed on us both. In retrospect, we had probably moved Terri home too early.

It was always our intention to bring her home permanently at some point, to make her part of our family again—that was essentially what our battle with Michael was about—but this was not the time. Much of the hope that had washed over me when she was at Vina del Mar was replaced by blackness. I held firm to our conviction that Terri would live with us again; still, there seemed a long journey ahead, and there were nights when, exhausted, I came close to despair, only to revive in the morning.

In the fall of 1990, Michael's sister-in-law, a nurse living in Philadelphia, called with exciting news. Two doctors, Yoshio Hosobuchi and Charles Yingling at the University of California at San Francisco, were experimenting with a new kind of brain surgery aimed at curing people with Parkinson's disease or traumatic brain injuries, people who had suffered lack of oxygen to the brain. (The medical term is *anoxia.*) We were electrified. Was there a chance that Terri ...?

At our urging, Michael contacted the university hospital to enlist Terri in the program. The procedure involved putting a stimulator in the brain, very much as doctors routinely put a pacemaker in the heart. Technically, Terri didn't qualify for the program, since her doctors didn't know the cause of her injury— she may or may not have suffered physical trauma, and she certainly didn't have Parkinson's. But in December, they agreed to accept her, and our spirits were lifted higher than they'd been at any time since her collapse. The doctors would speed her recovery. Perhaps she'd even learn to talk again, walk again—even live on her own, just like Bob's brother.

I didn't go with Michael and Terri because by then I had to take care of my mother at the nursing home. Michael was angry; he didn't want to go alone. Still, Michael reported the results. They were mixed. The operation didn't work as well as expected, but there was still noticeable improvement. Further rehabilitation was prescribed.

In January 1991, as a major part of Dr. Hosobuchi's prescribed follow-up program, Terri was admitted to MediPlex rehabilitation center in Bradenton, Florida. There, her admittance chart notes that she was saying "No" and "Stop" and "Mommy" because of the pain of her physical therapy.

Later, people said that Terri was in a persistent vegetative state from the moment she collapsed. The MediPlex notes are objective evidence that this isn't true. More, they gave us ample reason to believe that with rehabilitation, including speech therapy, she would have been able to say more, interact more. Tell us she loved us.

Because Terri was so obviously in pain during her therapy, MediPlex ordered a total bone scan on March 5, 1991, to determine its cause. The scan, which we only found out about some ten years later, revealed Terri had once broken her right femur, had suffered an "unusual" amount of rib injuries, and had sustained multiple other abnormalities to her skeleton. To the best of our knowledge, MediPlex did not investigate the radiologist's conclusion of trauma. We'll never know why they didn't report any of these findings of abuse to law enforcement authorities. As a guess, maybe they were afraid they'd be blamed for the injuries.

Why didn't Michael report the scan? He had to know about it, because on each of his visits he'd scrutinize Terri's medical charts. If he believed MediPlex was at fault, we believe he'd have sued them. But to do that would have meant making Terri's bone scan public. If we'd known about the scan when it was taken, we'd no doubt have been less trusting of Michael.

Another major element of Dr. Hosobuchi's follow-up program was for his associate, Dr. Yingling, to come to Florida to examine Terri. He determined Terri was improving and prescribed advanced rehabilitation. He recommended to Michael the Shands facility in Gainesville. We were ecstatic at Yingling's evaluation. I barely noticed the one-year anniversary of Terri's collapse. My spirits were good. Our Terri was going to get better.

Money remained a problem, especially during the fall of 1990. Michael was living on Terri's Social Security disability payments, and Bob was working, though not at the same financial level as in Pennsylvania, so it was a precarious existence. We were living from paycheck to paycheck and dared not think of what would happen if Terri suffered another cataclysmic event.

We might not have been able to care for Terri financially if the St. Petersburg community hadn't come to our rescue. Fundraisers were held on Terri's behalf, not only by our neighbors but also by Terri's co-workers at Prudential. There were bake sales, a Valentine's Day dance in her honor, a Terri Schiavo Day. Over Christmas, a mile-long line of candles placed on sandbags was set up along the seawall, and people could buy the bags as well as pray for Terri. Beyond the formal events, individual donations arrived from dozens of citizens, many of them strangers.

And here, publicly, we are finally able to thank everyone for their generosity, financial and spiritual. They sustained our efforts for Terri in a difficult time.

Altogether, some $50,000 was raised, money we used to pay for the plane trip to California, nurses, and other medical expenses. In the spring of 1991, we discovered that Michael had acquired a safety deposit box at a First Union Bank in St. Petersburg, in which he placed $10,000 in cash. We figured it probably came from the money raised in St. Petersburg, but Michael never said anything about it. From then on, we never got an accurate accounting of what he spent either on himself or on Terri.

According to Humana Northside's medical records, the doctors were mystified about the cause of Terri's collapse that horrible February 25, 1990. Like the paramedics, their first thought was a drug overdose, but the toxicology tests were negative. A congenital heart anomaly was ruled out by an echocardiogram which registered normal. A heart attack was considered, but no, Terri's enzymes weren't elevated. The only thing out of the ordinary was a low level of potassium in her blood.

Based on Dan Grieco's suggestion, Michael decided to investigate the possibility of suing Terri's ob-gyn, Dr. Stephen Igel, and her GP, Dr. Joel Prawer, for not having detected that Terri was in danger. Michael and I went together to the law firm of Woodworth and Dugan for the first of many conferences on the feasibility of a suit.

Glenn Woodworth hesitated, particularly since Michael's lawsuit against Prudential had failed (the suit was brought by a different lawyer in Woodworth's office). "There's no malpractice suit. There's nothing," he concluded. "Well, something happened to Terri," Bob said when we reported back. "Somebody did something wrong."

Woodworth called Gary Fox, a malpractice lawyer in Florida, and the two men came up with a strategy based on the presumption that Terri was bulimic. In November 1990, nine months after Terri's collapse, Woodworth filed at $20 million lawsuit against the two doctors on Terri and Michael's behalf. The sum was based on actuarial figures, which Woodworth later presented to the jury, that estimated the cost of Terri's medical and neurological treatment for the rest of her life, along with her rehabilitation.

Prawer and Igel had never tested Terri properly, Woodworth claimed. They'd been negligent. Neither Michael nor we nor any of Terri's friends had ever seen any sign of bulimia in Terri. Yet, as Bob said, *something* happened. *Somebody* was responsible.

What was to ensue broke my heart. The time I spent working with Michael to help Terri improve would soon seem a facade. What Michael wanted was to favorably influence the malpractice jury that he was a dedicated husband. When I realized this, I cried so much, I can still taste the tears.

The case went to trial in November 1992. Its outcome signaled a 180-degree turn in our relationship with Terri's husband. From being the closest of allies, united in our love for Terri and our desire to give her every chance at the best life possible, we became sudden enemies, bitter opponents in "The Schiavo Case" that divided the country as it divided Michael and us.

Chapter 6

Medical Malpractice

Q: (Glenn Woodworth): Why did you learn to become a nurse?

A: (Michael Schiavo): Because I enjoy it and want to learn more how to take care of Terri.

Q: You're a young man. Your life is ahead of you. When you look up the road, what do you see for yourself?

A: I see myself hopefully finishing school and taking care of my wife.

Q: Where do you want to take care of your wife?

A: I want to bring her home.

Q: If you had the resources available to you, if you had the equipment and the people, would you do that?

A: Yes, I would, in a heartbeat.

Q: How do you feel about being married to Terri now?

A: I feel wonderful. She's my life and I wouldn't trade her for the world. I believe in my wedding vows.

Q: You believe in your wedding vows. What do you mean by that?

A: I believe in the vows I took with my wife, through sickness, in health, for richer or poor. I married my wife because I love her and I want to spend the rest of my life with her. I'm going to do that.

Moving testimony from the 1992 trial, told with passion and conviction, accompanied by Michael's sobs and tears. Bobby and I were in the courtroom as Michael testified, and were deeply moved.

I imagined then that our son-in-law was feeling as much pain as I was. Michael said nothing about Terri's wish to die in case of a traumatic injury.

Michael had repeatedly told us that any money he won, and Terri won, from the lawsuits, would go toward her rehabilitation. When Terri came back from California and was living at MediPlex, Dr. Yingling urged us to move Terri to the Shands Hospital rehabilitation center in Gainesville.[1] Michael and we agreed that when and if Michael received an award, this would be our plan. Michael promised that Shands would be her next stop, for it was her best hope.[2]

We believed him, even though all through 1991-92 there were indications that Michael was neither the good husband nor the diligent caretaker he portrayed himself as being during the trial. In the summer of 1991, he transferred Terri from the MediPlex rehab center to the Sabal Palms nursing home in Largo, Florida. Michael told us Mediplex had recommended we discontinue rehab, that it made no sense to keep her there. This was the beginning of the end. From that point forward, Terri was denied any chance of improving. Tragically, she was never to receive any rehabilitation or therapy again. We were legally unable to stop him—we had, remember, given up our right to have a say in any medial decision regarding our daughter—but he told us he was doing it for her good, that he had investigated the nursing home and was convinced she

---

[1] Among the best in the nation, it is particularly famous for its work with brain-injured patients.

[2] In 2000, one of the jurors contacted Bobby in a rage. He had found out from press stories that Michael was trying to have Terri's feeding tube removed rather than trying to rehabilitate her. He said that he and the other jurors were suspicious of Michael from the start and that the only reason they awarded Terri any money was because they felt sorry for her.

would be well cared for until the medical malpractice money came through.

- It was in this period (September 1991) that he had the terrible fight with Suzanne.

- It was in this period that he began a relationship with a nurse named Cindy Shook.

- In May 1992, Michael moved out of our Vena del Mar house to live with his new girlfriend, Cindy Shook. Good, we thought. This would leave us free to take care of Terri.

- To our horror, he had Terri's two cats euthanized because Cindy had a dog and didn't want cats.

- In August, 1992, Terri's GP, Dr. Prawer,[3] on the advice of his insurance company, settled Michael's suit out of court for $250,000. The money was to go to Terri. Michael promised to add it to the malpractice lawsuit award—there would be that much more to spend on Terri's rehabilitation, he told us. But the money went elsewhere, and he never told us where.

All this should have made us more suspicious of our son-in-law. Yet so great were our dreams, and so persuasive Michael's assurances, that we simply waited for the trial to begin and focused on the victory we assumed would soon be ours. Our hope was that we'd get enough financing to take care of Terri at Shands—and then, when she was better, to bring her home for the rest of her life.

The verdict came quickly. Woodworth had asked for $20 million. The jury, evidently buying the argument that Terri was

---

[3] Dr. Prawer was later completely exonerated from any and all malpractice charges related to Terri.

bulimic but figuring that she herself was 70 percent at fault for her condition, awarded her $1.56 million and Michael $686,700 for loss of consortium. We were elated. Terri's financial problems had ended. We would be able to take care of her for as long as necessary. We could devote ourselves to her without worrying about the cost. As Michael said to me, "Mom, you and Dad [meaning Bob] and my mother and father will never have to worry again a day in your lives." If he said it once, he said it a thousand times.

A few weeks later, Bob went to Michael. "You made a commitment," he said. "If we got the money you were going to give Terri the therapy you promised. When is that going to be?"

"We'll talk about it later," Michael said.

Bob went to see him again a few days later with the same result.

On February 14, 1993, St. Valentine's Day, Bob and I went to the nursing home. Michael was in Terri's room, doing his homework for the nursing course he was taking. What happened next produced such deep emotional scars that even as I write this, twelve years later, I can feel our anger, relive the depths of our pain.

Bob started with his by-now-familiar plea. "Michael, your commitment. The promises you made to give Terri rehabilitation. When are you going to do that?"

"There's no money," Michael said coldly.[4]

"What do you mean there's no money? Terri got over a million dollars—and you said you were going to use it for her rehabilitation."

Michael was silent for a moment. Then, face contorted, eyes flashing disgust, he hurled his books across the room. "Look," he

---

[4] In a deposition he gave in 1999, Michael admitted saying this.

screamed. "I'm her husband. I'll make all the decisions. You have nothing to say."

He came after Bob physically, fists raised, wild with rage. "I thought we were going to tangle, and I was prepared to defend myself," Bob remembers.

Terrified, I had to jump in between the two of them to stop them from hurting each other.

"'You're a liar," Bob said.

Panting, his face bright red, the cords on his neck bulging, Michael glared at us. "This has nothing to do with you," he said. "This is about my wife, and as far as I'm concerned, you will never see your daughter again—that is, if I have anything to do with it." He turned around and stormed down the hall. "I'm calling my lawyer," he shouted.

And that was it.

The words, "you will never see your daughter again" hung in the room like poison gas. Then, too upset to see Terri, we drove home and told Bobby what happened. He put his hand through the wall.

"It was almost like I knew that was going to happen," Bobby says. "In fact, I had suggested even before the malpractice suit that we should sit down and get Michael to put everything in writing." (It was still a time when we trusted Michael, and Bob and I didn't think it was necessary.)

"Anyway, I ran out to the car. I was going to confront him. I was going to drive to his house, and I don't know what I would have done. And Mom came running after me, crying and begging me not to go, not to go. I was out of my mind, beyond reason, I was that mad. But I didn't go, which might have saved his life—or mine.

"One of the things that always upset me later was the questions the media asked all the time. 'What about the breakup? What about the split between the families?' Through his lawyer, George Felos, Michael would say, 'This wasn't about rehabilitation and therapy; this was about Mr. Schindler wanting his piece of the pie. He was demanding money from me and I wasn't going to give in to him.'

"Okay. Let's for a moment pretend that Dad was only after the money. That Dad was the worst person in the world. What bearing would it have on Michael's promise to use the money for rehabilitation and therapy? It doesn't take away the commitment he made to himself and to the jury—and to our family—that he was going to care for Terri for the rest of his life. And what does it have to do with his petitioning the courts to remove her feeding tube? It's as though he was saying, the father is a bad guy, therefore I'm going to kill his daughter."

That Valentine's Day was one of our darkest days. It was as though Michael had punched us in the stomach, taken our breath away. I thought of how my brother-in-law had been saved by the very rehabilitation Terri had been refused. She would exist at Sabal Palms nursing home with nothing but the most rudimentary care. No doctor, no therapist, no psychologist, would be allowed to try to make her better.

My thoughts went back to when she was a little baby and couldn't speak for herself. But as any mother, I knew when my baby needed help, and I was always there to ease her pain, mend her cuts and bruises, comfort her when she was sick. Now, though, her husband would not let anyone tell me if she was sick, let alone allow me to tend to her. It was unbearable.

Chapter 7
Sabal Palms

*A*lmost immediately—we think it was on Valentine's Day itself—Michael told the administrators at Sabal Palms not to release any medical information to us without his authority. He also instituted a "do not resuscitate" order.

On one of my visits to see Terri, she was sitting in the atrium looking pale and uncomfortable.

A nurse approached. "Gee, she looks kind of funny," I said.

"Well, you know, she just got back from the hospital."

No one had told us anything about a hospital, but I played along, figuring it was the best way to get information.

"Yes. But is she getting any better?"

"Absolutely! Do you remember that they took her gallstones out?"[1]

"Of course. It was in the spring."

"She's on antibiotics now," the nurse went on.

I thought I must be going mad. "That's great. What for?"

"She had a really bad urinary tract infection. But," she added cheerfully, "the antibiotics will cure it."

---

[1] In a later deposition, Michael used her gallstones against us, claiming that we cared so little about her that when she had her operation, we didn't bother to attend.

It was like being hit by lightning when we later found out that in June Terri had another UTI infection and that Michael had ordered Sabal Palms to refuse her any medication. The action was a potential death sentence. Untreated, the infection—sepsis—would spread throughout Terri's body and she would die. It is thanks to the people at the Sabal Palms, who countermanded Michael's wishes, that she survived. Without them, she might have died before we even knew she was in danger! The thought terrified me. We resolved to be more vigilant in the future—but how?

Bob made a direct plea to Michael in a letter:

July 16, 1993

Mike

Long before and during the malpractice trial, you made a number of commitments to Mary and myself. One of your commitments was that award money was to be used to enhance Terri's medical and neurological care ...

Since the trial and the ensuing award, you have chosen to ignore your commitments and have totally removed Terri from our lives. You have not communicated to us anything concerning her medical nor neurological status.

We want to know what Terri's latest evaluations are both medically and neurologically. It is very upsetting to be told by her medical attendants that you instructed them to withhold any and all information concerning our daughter's medical status ...

I/we are requesting you to keep us informed, on a weekly basis, of Terri's condition and progress. Simply drop us a note telling us what is happening. It will only take a few minutes. I am sure we will all sleep more comfortably.

On a long term basis, I would like you to consider giving Terri back to us, so we can give her the love and care she deserves. Logically and realistically you still have a life ahead of you.

Give this some thought. Are you ready to dedicate the rest of your life to Terri? We are! Let us know your feelings.

Mary and Bob Schindler

There was no reply.

Imagine what it's like to have your young and beautiful daughter in a nursing home in the first place. Then imagine that someone is controlling the information—or lack of it—you receive about her condition. Imagine what it's like to go to sleep (*if* you can sleep) without knowing whether your daughter is sick, whether there's been some crisis, whether her condition is stable or deteriorating. And imagine being in this position not just in one specific instance, but for twelve years.

No, don't imagine. I don't wish even the thought of it on anyone else.

Michael threatened Bob with a lawsuit, demanding return of $650 we "owed" him for household items he had contributed to our Vina del Mar living room. We felt it was a deliberate affront and decided to contest it. We hired a lawyer, Jim Sheehan, to represent us.[2] Sheehan was outraged by Michael's order to deny Terri medication. "This is wrong. He can't do that," he said, and promptly went after Michael's guardianship of Terri. Sabal Palms

---

[2] During his research on our behalf, Sheehan was informed by the nursing home that Michael had refused medication for Terri's UTI.

initially agreed to file a joint suit with us, but later backed off, giving as their excuse that there was so much evidence against Michael that we didn't need them.[3] In Michael's deposition for the case, responding to the question, "Why are you trying to kill her?" he answered, "Because I think it's what she'd want."

I think that's what she'd want. She had never said it *was* what she wanted. He was guessing at her wishes, and didn't state in open court that they *were* her wishes until 2000, when he was arguing for the removal of Terri's feeding tube. What she did and didn't want with regard to her death wasn't an issue in 1993. He would change his testimony seven years later, when the issue was at the core of our fight, and when it suited him.

The summer had passed almost without our noticing it. Before Terri's collapse, these months were a time for vacation, but now vacations of more than a couple of days were impossible. We kept working, occasionally went out to dinner, saw friends. Our world's boundaries were home and nursing home. Terri was always our primary concern.

In the fall of 1993, the court appointed an investigator named Novinski to try to determine Michael's fitness as Terri's guardian. After an inquiry of several weeks, he concluded Michael should be removed.

We were jubilant. If Michael were removed, he could no longer single-handedly dictate Terri's treatment. Judge Thomas Penick, who presided over the hearings, announced that he would appoint

---

[3] It's possible that pressure was put on them not to join the case, but that's only con-
jecture.

a guardian ad litem (an independent, interim guardian) and set a date two weeks later for the court to reconvene.

The guardian ad litem's name was John Pecarek. Judge Penick asked him if he had had an opinion on who the best permanent guardian might be. "Michael Schiavo," Pecarek stated firmly.

"Case closed," Penick declared, slamming his book closed, rising from the bench, and heading for the door.

"Wait a minute, Your Honor!" Jim Sheehan shouted after him. "You haven't even given me a chance to cross-examine him."

"It's closed," Penick said. "It's over." He walked out the door, Sheehan rushing after him to no avail.

Sheehan filed for a rehearing motion, but Penick denied it. The judge was right. The case was closed. What's more, the court ruled that all Michael's legal expenses were to be paid from Terri's medical fund, made up of the money he had won for her in the malpractice trial which he had pledged for her rehabilitation.

We felt abandoned, trapped in a court system where a judge can overturn the findings of his own investigator without explaining why and without giving the other side a chance to appeal. I was utterly bewildered. It was like watching frontier justice at work in an old western movie.

Some months later, we got a notice from Michael's lawyer asking if we wanted to pursue the case further. We called Sheehan. "There's nowhere to go with it," he said, and the case was permanently closed.

It was closed "with prejudice," Sheehan told us, but it was only much later that we learned what the term meant. Not only could we not question Penick's ruling ever again, but we could not refile, in any instance, to have Michael removed as guardian.[4]

We made so many mistakes in those first years! Lack of money was one reason: we simply couldn't afford lawyers' fees to pursue other avenues open to us. Optimism was another. Each time we went into court, or faced a hospital decision that went against Terri, we believed that justice would eventually triumph. After all, we were *right*—right to fight for Terri's well-being, right to insist on our say in her care, right that she deserved the best care and legal consideration. I in particular *knew* that everything would come out well. *How could anyone hurt Terri?* It was inhuman, inhumane, unthinkable.

We were so naïve.

Whenever we visited Terri at Sabal Palms, the nursing staff would complain to us about Michael's behavior. He bullied them and shouted at them when they did not obey his orders, to the point where the Sabal Palms administration tried to limit his access to Terri. Terry Russell, the administrator, had flatly refused to deny Terri medication, and we were led to believe that Sabal Palms had been inclined to join us in our suit against Michael's guardianship. As far as I was concerned, Terri might have been comfortable at Sabal Palms, but Michael wasn't. So in 1994, he moved Terri to the Palm Gardens nursing home in Largo, where he continued to warehouse her, and there was nothing we could do about it.

---

[4] In a hearing before Judge Greer over the question of having Terri's feeding tube removed, Sheehan testified that he had indeed never explained to us what the term meant and admitted he had made an error.

I fluctuate in my feelings toward Michael (much more than Bob, Bobby, or Suzanne), for I think back to the time at the beginning when Terri shone with love for him. For a long time, he was simply my son-in-law, part of the family. But it seemed to me then, and even more so now, that this moving of Terri was unconscionable.

Terri's transfer to Palm Gardens ensured, in effect, that Michael could do with Terri pretty much what he wanted, could keep back any medical information we sought.

Terri received no physical, speech, or occupational therapy at Palm Gardens during the five years she was there. She was washed, fed, dressed, put in a wheelchair in the morning, put down for a nap in the afternoon, put back in the wheelchair in the evening, and then put into bed for the night. I visited as often as I could. Most times, Terri would brighten when she saw me, grow dispirited when I left, but sometimes she gave no sign of recognition, made no movement to indicate she was aware of her surroundings. She simply sat passively, strapped to her chair, lost in a world no one could enter.

Those times made my heart ache. But then she would revive, and she became my daughter again—injured, God knows, but warm and sweet and precious. Alive to me, as I was to her.

We speak of the years 1994 to 2000 as the "lull" in Terri's case, the time from her transfer to Palm Gardens to Michael's suit to have her feeding tube removed. Our days routinely included visits to Terri, but we went to work, shared dinners and phone calls, and tried to remind ourselves that there were other aspects to our daily lives.

Still, neither side was inactive.

Michael certainly wasn't inactive in his personal life. Terri's girlhood friend Sue Kolb, now married and living in Pennsylvania, called me in July 1997.

"Did you see the obituary?" she asked.

"What obituary?"

"Michael's mother died."

"I'm sorry to hear it." I was. I'd always liked Claire, though I hadn't spoken to her since the rift between us and Michael.

"You know how in obituaries they always mention the siblings?"

"Of course."

"Well, this one says, 'survived by Michael Schiavo and his fiancée, Jodi Centonze.'"

I was appalled. Not only did the obituary not mention Terri, to whom Michael was still legally married,[5] but now he had a "fiancée." It made me sick at my stomach. We'd heard that Michael was living with another woman, and it made me sick. But to announce in the newspaper that he was going to marry her? That was too much.

All I could think of was how happy Terri was on her wedding day. Then I remembered Michael's using his wedding vows to make an impression on the medical malpractice jury. How hurt Terri would have been if she had known!

---

[5] If he'd divorced Terri, he would have lost access to her estate and guardianship.

Michael's handlers were busy on the legal front as well.

On August 23, 1997, we got a letter from a lawyer named George Felos announcing that the "court in your daughter's guardianship" had employed him "in the issue of withdrawal and/or refusal of medical treatment for your daughter." Felos quickly became Michael's champion. It is un-Christian not to love him, but I cannot do so. Felos might have been following Michael's wishes during the ensuing years when he argued for him, protected him, schemed for him, twisted truth for him. But we believe that it was Felos's strategy, not Michael's, that dictated the course that led to the death of my daughter. Maybe he had a political agenda—to become a spokesman for the euthanasia movement—and used Michael as his willing tool.

In 1995, some two years *before* he sent us the letter, Felos and Michael's guardianship lawyer, Deborah Bushnell, began to work out a legal strategy, almost surely for the removal of Terri's feeding tube. We know this because a court document (Bushnell's accounting of her costs) records at least one call between the two of them "*re* assistance with the analysis of life-prolonging procedures."

Ignorant of the Bushnell-Felos conversations, which might have superseded all other issues, we hired an attorney named Alan Grossman to argue to the courts that we should be able to obtain Terri's medical records, which had been cut off to us since 1993. It took him several months, but he finally prevailed, and the court granted us access to the medical information, though not to Terri's finances. That was the deal: medical records, yes; financial records, no.

It did us no good. I went to Palm Gardens armed with the court order and asked for the records. "I'm sorry," they said. "We can't release them without Mr. Schiavo's permission, and Mr. Schiavo says you cannot have any medical information."

I brandished the paper. "But I have a court order—"

They were implacable. "Sorry."

Bob called Grossman. "They're not honoring the order," he told the lawyer.

"That's terrible!" he said. "We'll have to file a suit and set up a hearing."

"A suit? A hearing? How much time would it take? How much would it cost?"

Grossman named a figure. I forget the exact amount, but we couldn't afford it. "We'll accumulate the money," Bob consoled me. But by the time we had enough money, the matter of Terri's medical records was submerged under far more important matters.

In May 1998, Michael filed a petition with the probate court to have Terri's feeding tube removed.

Just writing that sentence brings back the horror of the moment we found out about it: August 23, 1997. I remember thinking that this couldn't be coming from Michael, my son-in-law. Seven years earlier, he had fought side by side with me for her recovery; a husband who loved his wife could not conceivably petition for her death. Bob felt like someone had sucker-punched him in the stomach. Michael was trying to murder his daughter! Like Suzanne, he thought Michael was sick to even consider such a petition.

Still, the petition *did* come from Michael, and I could feel my heart harden toward him. *He* might not love her enough to try to get her better, I thought, but her family did.

I thought of what Michael did to Terri's cats when he wanted them out of the way. Now, Terri! I couldn't sleep for a week. Every time I closed my eyes, I could see Terri looking at me, begging for my help. Eating made me sick. Maybe it was my unconscious saying I shouldn't eat if my little girl was going to be starved. I reassured myself that no judge would ever allow anyone to die of starvation. The thought did little to ease my pain.

The case didn't come into court until January 2000, perhaps because the court was waiting for the Florida Legislature to enact a law, championed by Felos, allowing feeding tubes to be declared artificial life support. (The feeding tube was the only "support" Terri needed, and to us it was as though the law was tantamount to declaring IVs artificial life support, which would put a whole lot of not very sick patients in danger of having them removed.)

By that time we had hired a lawyer, Pamela Campbell, to represent us, and her optimism heartened us. Still, this was a terrible time. I can't possibly convey the anxiety we continued to feel or the pain of arising each morning thinking, *They're trying to kill our Terri.*

Until 2000, we were an ordinary family afflicted with a private tragedy. Now, however, we were about to plunge into a five-year siege in which the name Terri Schiavo became known throughout the world. And our lives—psychological, professional, philosophical, and emotional—would be transformed forever.

Chapter 8

Permission Granted

A friend of Bobby's knew George Greer, the judge who would preside over Michael's application to have Terri's feeding tube removed. "He's a good man," Bobby's friend said a few days before the trial was to begin. "A man of God. He has a good reputation. I think it'll be a fair trial."[1]

We were sure that as soon as he heard our arguments, Judge Greer would throw the case out; nevertheless, I was sick with worry, and so was Bob, whose high blood pressure—a threat all his life—was acting up again. The tension was relentless. *A judge, a stranger, was going to decide whether Terri lived or died.* It seemed to me unfair and unfeeling. Judge Greer didn't know Terri. And now we were told that his word could take her from us? Insane!

The hearing, which would run for five days, started on January 24, 2000, in Clearwater. At Felos's request, the venue had been moved from St. Petersburg to Clearwater, which was the lawyer's home turf. Felos had been working on the case from 1995 forward, so he really had a chance to prepare himself. We didn't think much preparation was necessary for our side; we were sure to win. Felos was just a name to us then. We didn't know he specialized in euthanasia cases. We didn't know how dangerous he was.

---

[1] We asked Judge Greer to see Terri for himself, but he refused. As far as we know, he never visited her during the five years of court hearings.

The courtroom reminded Bobby of one he had seen in the movie *The Verdict*, all high ceilings and large windows, with scarred wooden pews and jurors' chairs. (There would be no jurors present at the hearing, of course; the decision would be Judge Greer's alone.) We were represented by attorney Pamela Campbell, who, attended by her assistant, was delighted with the Southern-type setting. "The perfect ambiance," she told us.

Michael arrived with George Felos and Felos's wife, Constance; also a lawyer, she often worked with him. Bob, Suzanne, Bobby, and Bobby's girlfriend, Lori Stewart, arrived with me; Michael's father and his father's lady friend came with Michael. Bobby and Lori had faxed a letter to the press about the abomination being perpetrated on Terri—perhaps a public outcry would stop it, they thought. Only the local ABC channel and a reporter from the *St. Petersburg Times* showed up. So the courtroom, which seemed to me cavernous and menacing, was virtually deserted.

Judge Greer entered. He was a slight man, about five-six or five-seven and balding, looking more like a CPA than a judge, and as I watched him take his seat, I prayed that he would be just and wise and would spare Terri.

The first day was devoted to the opening arguments. Michael and Felos had to prove two things in order for the feeding tube to be removed: that Terri would wish it and that Terri was in a persistent vegetative state under Florida law. In her opening statement, to our amazement, Pamela acknowledged that Terri was PVS. *But that's half our case!* we wanted to scream. Her rationale for this tactic was that she wasn't sure she could find a doctor who would disagree with that diagnosis, and that if we were to bring in a doctor to examine Terri, Felos would be present at the examination and could use against us any negative finding the doctor might make. In retrospect, however, not bringing in our own doctor was a terrible mistake.

As for Terri's wishes: Felos's contention that she'd expressed them stunned us. She hadn't! There was no evidence for it! Surely she'd have mentioned such wishes to her parents, her siblings, or her friends at one time or another over the years. But no one could recall her saying anything about them at any time. Yes, Michael would testify that Terri had expressed a wish to die if she was incapacitated, contrary to what he said in his November 1993 deposition, but what judge would decide against Terri on the basis of one man's word—and a man with his own agenda, at that?

We had given our depositions the previous September, simple, unembellished statements that Terri had shown undeniable signs of awareness, that she could follow us with her eyes, that she could laugh and move, and that she was even capable of swallowing baby food. George Felos had taken the depositions, and I found him cordial.

But we were unprepared for what we should say in our depositions to counteract what Michael's was likely to say, and unprepared for the hearing itself. Bob had half assumed Greer would throw the case out, particularly in view of a recent interim guardian's report.

Prior to the trial, another guardian ad litem was appointed to investigate the merits of Michael's guardianship, a man named Richard Pearse. He recommended that Terri's feeding tube be kept in. He felt that Michael had huge conflicts of interest—the disposition of Terri's estate, for example—and wondered why Michael had waited seven years to assert her wish to die. In a long document rebutting Pearse's opinion, Felos filed an objection to the report before the trial started. The report was thrown out. In the ensuing five-year period, Judge Greer acted as Terri's guardian ad litem.[2] Yet I still believed that in the end no one would allow Terri to be starved to death.

So, untutored, defenseless, as naïve as ever, we appeared unarmed—naked—in Judge Greer's court. We were to pay for our ignorance.

Michael's side went first—they were the claimants. Bobby and Suzanne were kept sequestered in the jury room, so they didn't hear Michael's testimony, or that of any of his witnesses, though we, as the opposite party in the suit, were allowed to listen.

I was the first witness for our side, and I was a terrible. I had never been in court before, to say nothing of testifying in a case that was to decide whether my daughter lived or died, so I was extremely nervous. And Felos, who had been so polite during the deposition, attacked savagely. He pointed out discrepancies between my deposition and what I was saying now, minor points that he hammered relentlessly. *He's trying to make me out a liar*, I thought, and I became more and more defensive, more and more confused.

Pamela Campbell did not object to either his tactics or to his questions. Felos kept going after me and going after me, and I knew what I was saying was the truth, but he made it sound as if my

---

[2] This disturbed many of the attorneys who studied the case, who felt one of the appeals courts should have overturned Greer's decision, since he was acting as Terri's guardian. That Terri was never afforded a guardian who wasn't also the judge in her case, and that she was never afforded her own attorney, was in direct violation of Florida statute law.

testimony were all lies. In my deposition, I had told him that Terri, then aged seventeen or eighteen, was upset over the fact that Karen Ann Quinlan had been taken off life support.[3] At the trial, Felos pounced. He showed me some newspapers.

Q: (Felos): These are ... pages from the *St. Petersburg Independent* dated September 13, 1975; September 18, 1975; April 1, 1976; and May 24, 1976, regarding the Karen Ann Quinlan Case.

The first one, September 13, 1975, has the headline regarding the case, "Father Asks the Judge to Let His Daughter Die." What was Terri's birthday?

A: (Me): 12/3/63.

Q: December of 1963?

A: Yes.

Q: Well, when this headline broke, Terri would have been 11 years old. And she also would have been, in the next headline September 18—September 23, 1975, *Your World Today*, about the Karen Ann Quinlan case, "To Live or Die," Terri would have been 11 at that time.

Then I would like to bring your attention to the front page of the *St. Pete Times*. Terri would have just turned 12 years old, which has on the front page, "Quinlan Has Right to Die," which is when the Supreme Court of New Jersey ruled in favor of the parents to remove the ventilator.

And the last one in May of 1976, again front page of the *St. Pete Times*, "Quinlan Respirator Turned Off." Now you mentioned you had these conversations with Terri in response to the Karen Ann Quinlan case as the parents were trying to remove the respirator, but Terri was not 17 or 18 years old at the time, was she?

A: No.

---

[3] Quinlan's case became a national story.

Q: At that time, Terri was 11 years old?

A: Yes.

Q: Is it your testimony that you had conversations with your 11-year-old daughter regarding artificial—removal of artificial life support?

A: But the Karen Ann Quinlan case went on for years.

Q: Ma'am, your testimony was that you had these conversations with your daughter when it was front page in the newspaper, when it was newsworthy, and when the parents were trying to remove the respirator. The respirator was removed in May of 1976, when your daughter was 12. My question is, are you saying that you had conversations with your daughter, the conversations you alluded to with your daughter, occurred when she was 11 and 12 years old? You have to speak out loud so the court can hear you.

A: Yes.

Q: Well now, again, *what* do you say that Theresa said about the Karen Ann Quinlan case to you.

A: "Just leave her alone."

Q: Now I took your deposition last August and on Page 28, Line 1, I asked you, "Now did you discuss with Terri the issue of whether the respirator should be removed?" We were talking about the Karen Ann Quinlan case. [You said], "I really don't remember. I don't remember exactly what was said."

A: Yes.

Q: Okay. Was that testimony you gave in your deposition truthful? That you don't exactly remember what was said?

A: Yes.

Humiliated and utterly confused, I thought maybe I had gotten it wrong, that Terri wasn't upset about Karen Ann Quinlan, that it was somebody else.

It turns out that it *was* Karen Ann Quinlan whom Terri was upset about. Quinlan was taken off her respirator on the order of her father, and seven years later, there was a television show on the case that Terri had seen when she was eighteen. But I was so intimidated that my brain stopped working, and Felos could do what he wanted with me.

Bob watched me in agony. "He had you totally confused," he told me afterwards. "You didn't know what you were saying. I gave Pam Campbell a shot in the ribs and told her to stop Felos from torturing you, but she didn't."

Bob's testimony was a classic case of the accused accusing the accuser. In his deposition, Bob had begun firing questions at Felos. Felos, furious, said, "*I'll* ask the questions," and went at Bob with a barrage of hypothetical questions about the conditions under which Bob would allow Terri to die.

Felos brought up the same questions at the trial. "What if Terri had her arms cut off and her legs cut off, would you still want her to live like that?" "What if she had open heart surgery?" He was obviously trying to box Bob into a corner, trying to get him to admit there would be instances when the right course would be to remove Terri's feeding tube, but Bob kept insisting that these were hypothetical questions, and he refused to answer them, pointing out that there were seven definitions of the word, "hypothetical," and which one did Felos mean? Judge Greer made Bob answer.

"I was belligerent the whole time," Bob said later. "I made a fool out of myself doing it. At the trial I said, 'If you remember, Felos, I told you that before I'd make any decision like that, I'd have to give it a lot of thought, bring in a team of doctors.'"[4]

Bobby also spoke for our side:

"Felos's wife, Constance, did some of the questioning for Michael's side, Pamela Campbell for ours," he remembers. "Pamela wanted to establish that Terri and I had a conversation about her desire to divorce Michael. Felos himself stood up and said, 'Objection. Hearsay evidence.' And the judge sustained it. And I'm sitting there thinking to myself, *This whole case is based on hearsay evidence. Why is there no objection to Michael's statements about Terri's alleged death wishes? Clearly that was hearsay evidence.* It was incredible."

"They kept me till last," Suzanne says, "and I always think they did that on purpose because Michael didn't like me. They made me sit outside by myself in that jury room, day after day, saying they were going to call me—but they never did, not until the end of the week.

"I didn't testify for long, and I don't remember it all any more, but Felos started asking me about my ex-husband at the time Terri collapsed. He was trying to make the case that I was jealous about Terri and Michael starting a family. Pam objected, and I remember the judge sustained it, because it was totally irrelevant. I remember thinking, *What does that have to do with anything?* What *did* mean something was whether I knew Terri's wishes, and of course

---

[4] In an appearance on *Larry King Live*, Michael used Felos's hypothetical questions to attack Bob. "Well, if you listened to Mr. Schindler in the testimony back in the trial, he would cut off his daughter's arms and legs and still keep her alive, and I'm not going to let any parent that would do that to their child ever take care of her." The public thought we were fanatical nuts who'd go to ridiculous extremes to save Terri's life. Say what you will about Felos, he was certainly a master manipulator.

she had never expressed anything like wanting to die if she was incapacitated—so I said so."

Our star witness was Terri's friend Jackie Rhodes.[5] Calm, unintimidated by Felos, she testified that Terri was very unhappy in her marriage and wanted to leave Michael.

Jackie talked of the pressure she was under not to say so:

Q: (Pam Campbell): Did you attend the trial in this case? The malpractice trial?

A: (Jackie Rhodes): Yes, I attended the malpractice trial. A few other people from work also attended to tell what kind of person Theresa was and she was a loss to the company, and you know, to her family and friends.

One thing that did occur during the trial, my husband was in the hospital having a heart cauterization and I had to go down there as soon as I left the courtroom, as soon as I testified, and the malpractice attorney followed me down to the pay phone and said to me, you know, it wouldn't help the case at all if I told them Theresa and Michael were talking about getting a divorce. I turned to him and I said if I'm asked the question and that is the correct answer, that is the answer I'm going to give.

She *was* asked.

Q: Do you know whether or not Terri specifically was seeking to get a divorce?

A: She had talked about it on several occasions. As a matter of fact, we had talked about living together, as my husband was very controlling to me and he asked for, my husband asked for a divorce also.[6]

---

[5] Terri's other good friend Diane Meyer also testified—about the fight she had with Michael in Pennsylvania.

[6] Jackie and her husband divorced soon after Terri collapsed.

And she talked about Terri's condition:

Q: What were your observations of Terri then?[7]

A: Terri always responded when I went to see her. I would come in and say, Terri, it's Jackie. How are you? I would startle her and I learned not to do that. She would just jump a little bit. Then I would talk to her if I were standing by her bed.

And in talking to her, her eyes would always look at me. There were times that she seemed to be a little tense with her arms up like this. And when I would talk to her and tell her who I was, it seemed as though her arms would relax and move down during our visit.

Q: Did you notice any other specific reactions or changes in facial expression?

A: Sometimes it was she would make sounds depending on maybe what I would say to her.

Jackie said that she and Terri had talked about living together after they had separated from their husbands. She described Michael's controlling nature, about his checking Terri's odometer, about his belittling Terri in public.

She also swore that Terri and Michael had fought bitterly the day before Terri collapsed. Terri had called her in tears, saying that Michael was furious she had spent so much money on her hair. Jackie asked if Terri wanted her to come over—she was worried because Terri was so upset—but Terri said no, she could handle it alone.

Jackie talked movingly about Terri's visits to my mother in the nursing home. Jackie would sometimes go with her. They saw many old people hooked up to respirators and other machines; surely this

---

[7] 1996, Jackie had moved from Florida and came back to see Terri.

was the time Terri would have talked about ending her own life if she were in that condition, but she did not.

I could back up what Jackie was saying. When Terri and I visited Mom together, she never mentioned any wish to die in similar circumstances. Terri would bring the other patients gifts and flowers. *Her goal was to keep them alive!* I kicked myself for not having said this during my own testimony.[8]

Jackie's presence was difficult for me. Here was a passionate, vibrant girl about Terri's age, a girl who was as good a friend as anyone could have been, as loyal to Terri as Terri would have been to her if their situations had been reversed. But they *weren't* reversed. Jackie had a full life ahead of her. Terri's would be limited in her abilities to move and to talk. I didn't resent Jackie, but I couldn't help making the comparison.

Michael's testimony centered on his assertion that Terri had indeed expressed a wish to be taken off life support if she was unable to care for herself. There was nothing surprising here. The surprise came in this exchange:

Q: (George Felos): Mr. Schiavo, you mentioned that your mother passed away. When did that occur?

A: (Michael Schiavo): July 1997.

Q: Did that experience, at all, affect your decision to bring this petition?

A: My mother gave me a gift when she was dying. We stopped her feeding because that's what she wanted—and her medication. She gave me the gift that it's okay to die.

---

[8] In Judge Greer's ruling, he cited every one of the witnesses' testimony except Jackie's. None of us knows why.

It was the reason, he said, that he decided it was time to remove Terri's feeding tube.

But in May 1997, two months before Claire Schiavo died, Felos is on record with the court asking for money to pursue Michael's wish to remove the feeding tube. And Michael later admitted that he and Felos were speaking about the removal in 1996:

Q: (Felos): Your current petition to remove artificial life support was filed in May of 1988 [*sic*]. Why did you wait two and a half years to file the petition.

A: (Michael): I met you in the beginning of 1996, I believe. I was talking to another attorney.

Q: Well, okay. I have to caution you not to testify as to any communication you might have with your attorney because of attorney/client privilege. Did you put into motion your decision to remove the feeding tube before the petition was filed in May of 1988 [*sic*]? ... When did you make the decision and start putting it in motion?

A: In 1995. End of 1995.

There was another surprise, this one from the deposition Michael gave before the 2000 trial:

Q: (Campbell): Have you considered turning over the guardianship to [Robert and Mary] Schindler?

A: (Michael): No, I have not.

Q: And why?

A: I think that's pretty self-explanatory.

Q: I'd like to hear your answer.

A: Basically, I don't want to do it.

Q: And why don't you want to do it?

A: Because they put me through pretty much hell the last few years.

Q: Can you describe what you mean by hell?

A: The litigation they put me through.

Q: Any other specifics besides litigation?

A: Just their attitude towards me because of the litigations. There is no other reason. I'm Terri's husband and I will remain guardian.

It took Felos to rescue him:

Q: (Felos): You were also asked a question about resigning as guardian or would you consider doing that. Upon reflection, is there anything that you want to add in response to that question?

A: (Michael): Yeah. Another reason would be that her parents wouldn't carry out her wishes.

Michael's testimony in 2000, given with all the passion and tears he had mustered for the malpractice suit in 1992, convinced me he was a fine actor, but failed to persuade me he was telling the truth.

Another surprise came in the form of the "corroborating" witnesses Felos called in on the matter of Terri's wish to die: Scott Schiavo, Michael's brother, and Joan, Michael's sister-in-law. Both of them quickly backed Michael's statement, and were dismissed.

We thought their testimony was ridiculous. For one thing, they were rushed in at the last minute; for another, their testimony was hearsay; for a third, Scott's testimony cited different, contradictory versions of Terri's wishes, and Joan never specified what Terri's wishes were. Finally—and this was a question that applied to Michael himself as well—why had they waited ten years to say anything about Terri's wishes? They hadn't been deposed, and

Pam Campbell had no material with which to prepare her cross-examination.[9]

By the time they testified, there was a fairly large audience, including a few members of the press, some of our family and friends—and Brian Schiavo, another of Michael's brothers, who was then called to testify. At this, several people in the courtroom stood up and yelled to Pam, "He's been sitting here the whole week long! He's heard all the testimony. He can't testify." Pam asked that Brian be disqualified, and Judge Greer upheld her objection.[10]

Michael's side called other witnesses. One was a neurologist, Dr. James Barnhill, who said that Terri was PVS and would not get better. (It made me all the sadder that Pam had advised us not to have a doctor examine Terri for purposes of the hearing, so that Barnhill could be refuted.) Another was Beverly Tyler who had taken a "regional poll" for a research center in Atlanta and found that most people said that if they were like Terri they would not want to live in her condition.

Such polls—and there many conducted about the case over the next five years—made us furious. The responders did not know the specifics of "her condition." And who can say what they'd do in actual circumstances? It's easy to talk about giving up life if you're healthy enough to answer a poll. But at what point in an illness, or at what degree of pain, do you say, "That's it"—an irrevocable decision? "I wouldn't want to be a burden to my caregivers," many respondents say.[11] In Terri's case, we *know* that she would have

---

[9] We could have provided uncles, aunts, cousins, and additional friends of Terri's who were lined up to testify that Terri made no such comments, but Pam chose not to call them.

[10] To get Brian's testimony on record, Felos later questioned Brian in front of the court recorder when Judge Greer was absent.

[11] Life is never a burden, regardless of a person's disability.

wanted to live, because she would have found her life surrounded by the people who loved her, and because she would know how much we wanted her with us.

A different witness upset us profoundly. On the second or third day we came to the courthouse, Bob approached a Catholic priest, Father Gerard Murphy, sitting outside the courtroom and, thinking the priest was there to offer us support, thanked him for coming. But Father Murphy had arrived to testify on Michael's behalf. He had never spoken to anyone in our family, had never gone to visit Terri, and did not know that Terri was a practicing, faithful Catholic who had gone to Mass the day before her collapse. He had gotten all his information about Terri from Felos, who introduced him at the trial as the official spokesman for the Catholic Church on end-of-life matters—in fact, I didn't think he could appear without permission from his bishop, Robert Lynch.[12] It didn't seem to bother him that Michael had been cohabiting with someone for five or so years, just that Terri was disabled and wouldn't want to live with her disabilities, though of course he never heard her say so.

He testified that part of his ministry work was visiting old-age homes and nursing homes to comfort and bless the people who were dying. The Church, he announced, condoned the termination of a human life by removing life support and would indeed permit the removal of Terri's feeding tube.

We had not known Father Murphy would testify, or how he would testify; we could have produced a dozen priests who would have refuted him. But attorney Campbell called no one and did not ask for help.

---

[12] He remains our bishop today.

After the hearing was over, we all went to see Bishop Lynch himself. Bobby pleaded with the bishop to say that Father Murphy was wrong about Church teaching, that his testimony set a false legal precedent, and to publicly speak out about what was happening to Terri. Bishop Lynch refused. We believe that if he had intervened, if he had testified that the Church opposed the taking of life in any form, if he had asked his priests to mobilize the hundreds of thousands of parishioners in the St. Petersburg area to say that Terri was a human being even though badly injured, the entire trial might have ended differently, and Terri might be alive today. But Bishop Lynch ignored us. He turned his back.

Catholicism had been ingrained in me from the moment I was born. Now I felt betrayed, not by Catholicism itself, but by its representatives in St. Petersburg. Bob, Bobby, and Suzanne were enraged at the bishop for his hypocrisy. I was saddened. It seemed to me that the Church was deserting my daughter, and it was only God Who could tell me why.

Much later, Bobby put together an editorial regarding the bishop's disregard for the Catholic Church's teaching, and his responsibility, as Terri's chief pastor, to defend not only her life but the sanctity of all human life:

I am a professed Roman Catholic man striving to be a good Christian. I believe in the teachings of the Catholic Church and I have a deep respect for our Holy Father, Pope John Paul II. However, I struggled profoundly with my faith and trust in the Church after Father Murphy's testimony in which he stated that to remove my sister's feeding tube depriving her of nutrition and hydration, causing her death, was morally acceptable according to Church teaching. Furthermore, our local bishop of the Diocese of St. Petersburg, Bishop Robert

Lynch, refused to correct this grave misconception of Church teaching and basically said, "It's Michael Schiavo's decision to make" and stated that the Church would not get involved.

I was devastated and angry. How could this be? I may not be a theologian or Church scholar, but I know that to remove my sister's feeding tube deliberately to cause her death is euthanasia and is forbidden by the Church as stated in our *Catechism*. ... Why did Bishop Lynch not rise to Terri's defense? Why did he not defend her inherent right to life? How could he stand in direct conflict with the clear teaching of the Catholic Church, and how can he remain as a bishop after having done so? Terri was a practicing Roman Catholic woman, and he should have been the one to shepherd and defend her. "He is her Bishop!" I thought to myself. "How can he abandon her?"

It wasn't only Bishop Lynch who disappointed us. In 2004, my family sent a letter to every Catholic bishop of every diocese in the United States asking them to publicly speak out about what was happening to Terri. We received only three affirmative responses.

When Felos spoke of Terri as though he knew her, or knew what she wanted—as though they were friends—it drove Bobby crazy.

"I'm sitting there thinking, *He has no idea who Terri is. None whatsoever.* I got so mad one time that I stormed out of the courtroom, and I hit the door so hard I actually snapped my watch in half. If Terri had known what was going on, she'd have been the first one to tell Felos to go to hell. She'd have been fighting just as hard for us as we were fighting for her. The notion that Felos and Terri had some type of alliance—that he knew her mind—it was absolutely the furthest thing from the truth, and so infuriating that I thought I'd get thrown out of the courthouse."

Felos called another witness, Judge Greer's appointed guardian ad litem, Richard Pearse. "If you had known that Scott Schiavo and Joan Schiavo had heard Terri Schiavo's request to have her life ended under extreme circumstances, would you have reported as you did?" Felos in effect asked Pearse. "If you had known of Beverly Tyler's poll or Dr. Barnhill's findings, or Scott and Joan Schiavo's testimony, would your mind have changed?"

His answer was disturbing. "My mind would possibly have changed."

Reflecting on the hearing later, Suzanne summed up what we were all feeling:

"As the week went on, we become more and more frustrated, more and more upset. I mean, we went through a week of hell. In the beginning, we were concerned, but we still felt pretty good. But when it was over, I felt like we were all run over by a truck. I mean, it was a hellacious week. Hellacious in that we heard testimony from Michael's sister-in-law and brother—and then the priest—that was just incorrect. We were all blown away by the priest. We couldn't believe it.

"It's frustrating to hear people saying things you know are untrue and you can do nothing about it. You want to stand up and say, 'That's not true,' because you know in your heart that it's not. And they're people taking an oath on the Bible!"

Like Suzanne, Bob was stunned at the testimony of Michael's relatives.

"I kept thinking, *Right will prevail*, because everything we said was true and everything they said was dishonest. I believed in the theory that honesty and truth prevail. Greer's a judge. He'll rule in our favor. But these people put their hand on the Bible and immediately said things we're sure weren't true. I couldn't believe that was actually happening."

Bobby suffered as much after the trial as during it. "There were moments when I thought there was no way we were going to lose, and there were moments when I thought, *He's going to rule against us.* I hardly slept for two weeks. The night before the decision, I didn't sleep at all. It was just a horrible two weeks, waiting for the decision to come in. And I must have talked over the phone every day for probably hours at a time, just rehashing the case over and over with my dad. I didn't know what to think. I remember just going back and forth. I remember what my parents said: 'Our family's made a lot of mistakes, but the one thing we don't do is lie.' I was asked, why not testify and lie that Terri had expressed a wish to live? I said no, because if we had, we would have been like them. In point of fact, we turned away a man who offered to produce an unimpeachable forgery of Terri's living will in which Schiavo's claims would have been contradicted.

"I taught in a Catholic school, and I taught my students that honesty is everything. I think we all like to think that at the end of the day, because we were truthful, and honest, we would prevail based on that. And that the judge would see we were being honest. But it didn't happen."

I saw the trial somewhat differently. Of course I was unhappy with the way it went, them lying and me knowing they were lying. But at the end of the trial, I thought to myself, *I know all this happened and I know the trial didn't go well, but there is no way that anybody is going to starve a human being to death.*

That's all I kept thinking. Over and over, that's all I kept thinking.

Chapter 9

The Fight for Terri's Life

$\mathcal{W}$e tried to keep up our regular lives. Suzanne was a stockbroker for TD Waterhouse by day and a wife and mother at night. Bobby taught school at Tampa Catholic High School. I was working at the Hallmark store on St. Peter beach. Bob was working under contract for an engineering firm. But the suspense of waiting for Greer's decision pervaded every minute of all our lives.

Just after noon on February 11, 2000, two weeks after the trial ended, Bob got a call from Pam Campbell's paralegal, Teresa Muhlstadt, asking us to come to Pam's office in the Alexander Building in St. Petersburg. Greer had made his decision, and Pam wanted to tell us about it in person. It's a ten- to fifteen-minute drive from our house, and I don't remember either of us saying a word. Neither before nor after, in the entire time frame of our daughter's ordeal, can I remember being so anxious, so scared.

When we pulled up in front of the building, to my astonishment there must have been eight or nine cameras poking at us, and reporters' indistinct questions buzzed around us like mosquitoes. By this time, to the local press at least, Terri's fate was a big story. The media presence was like a dress rehearsal for what came later.

Teresa had come outside and held the press back. I looked at her face. She said nothing, but her expression gave her away. We had lost.

No! My heart screamed. I couldn't believe it. Maybe I was wrong. Maybe Pam would have good news. I couldn't look at Bob. Had he guessed what I guessed?

Teresa led us upstairs to Pam's office. She had also notified Bobby and Suzanne that the decision was coming. Bobby was already in the office, having gotten there with his childhood friend Steven Meyer just before the fax came announcing Greer's verdict. Suzanne arrived moments after we did. Pam turned to us and shook her head. "He's allowing the feeding tube to come out."

At first, I was numb. Then, quickly, I started to cry and couldn't stop. I cried and cried as if the dam I had built inside me had broken and nothing could build it back again. I thought I would cry forever.

Pam and Teresa were crying, too. My family was beside me, and they must have been crying as well, but I was only conscious of Pam and Teresa. Pam said, "Don't worry, don't worry. We'll appeal, we'll appeal." That's all she kept saying for a long time.

I hadn't thought of an appeal. I thought that the judge had ordered the feeding tube removed, and that would be that. That Terri's tube would be taken out that day. I mean, I was hysterical. Pam said, "It's not going to happen today. It's not going to happen tomorrow. Just settle down and don't worry." Then she tried to explain what the process would be, but I could understand none of it, not even that there was still hope.

Bobby was in almost as bad shape. "Before the fax came in, my anxiety was so profound I felt I was going to faint. When it did come, it was an absolute shock. I didn't know what it meant. I mean,

I did know, but I didn't know the time frame. I didn't know how long we had. I didn't know if we had a week, a month, a year—I just didn't know. And that's what was most scary: I just didn't know."

Pam sat there and read Greer's decision to us, but to this day, I've never read it myself. I've read sections of it, but never the whole thing. I can barely even look at a copy. When I see the date, I relive the day, and no one should be asked to do that.

After we had quieted a little—when I could breathe again without choking—Pam told us we'd have to look for attorneys better able to handle the appeal process. We were all relieved. Pam is a fine, sympathetic woman. Her newly established law practice was like that of a medical general practitioner, whereas what we needed now was a specialist, someone who specialized in euthanasia cases like Felos.

We left her office, incapable of further discussion or of making plans. Bobby and Steven stayed behind to handle the media so they could thank our supporters for us. But for me, the moment Judge Greer had rendered his decision, the future became a black hole.

The day after the decision, we went with Bobby, his girlfriend Lori, Suzanne, and her six-year-old daughter Alex—to whom we had promised the outing—to the Florida State Fair. I remember thinking, *How do you explain to a six-year-old that a judge ordered her aunt to be put to death?* Terri hadn't committed any crime. Alex had visited her. She had seen her smile and laugh. She knew she was sick. I thought it best not to tell her anything, to let her enjoy herself at the fair.

I don't remember anything about the fair itself, except that I was afraid I'd never make it through the day. My legs were weak, and a couple of times I thought I was going to faint. Bob remembers walking through the fair but, overwhelmed by thoughts of what had happened the day before, nothing else. I was trying not to think at all, to blank my brain to stop Pam's voice, the memories of the trial, the visions of Terri, from creeping in. It didn't work.

On that day, Bob got a call from a woman named Jana Carpenter, who had introduced herself to him during the trial, which she had attended during its last two days.

"It was a Saturday when the call came in," Bob says. "Jana told me she belonged to a group of doctors, nurses, caretakers, and attorneys. 'There are some doctors who would like to visit Terri at the Palm Gardens nursing home,' she said. 'Do you think you could arrange it?'

"Three doctors showed up and spent an hour with Terri. Based on what they saw of her, each filled out affidavits confirming that Terri could swallow and that she was not in a persistent vegetative state.

"I should have been happy, but to me it was a case of locking the barn door after the horses had fled. They gave the affidavits to Pam Campbell,[1] who immediately filed an emergency petition with Judge Greer. Meanwhile, I got another affidavit from a retired bishop, Thomas Larkin, Bishop Lynch's predecessor, who, I guess, had come to the trial after hearing of Father Murphy's testimony. He was accompanied by Monsignor Thaddeus Malanowski, a

---

[1] We had been unable to locate an appeals lawyer in so short a time.

retired Army general and Catholic priest.[2] Bishop Larkin's affidavit stated that Father Murphy had misrepresented the Catholic Church's position on end-of-life matters, and Pam included that in her package to Greer."

The motion for rehearing, which was heard by Judge Greer on March 2, 2000, asked for a review of the case and for Greer to allow medical tests for Terri to determine her capabilities and true neurological condition. On March 7, he denied all motions in the petition.

By then, though, the depressed lethargy we were battling had lifted. We were mad. Our energy returned. We renewed our commitment to Terri that we would get her the therapy she so desperately needed. By God, we would fight for our daughter's life! If she had to die, we would not let it happen quietly as we suspect our adversaries had planned.

Michael was fighting, too. Shortly after our doctors examined Terri, he filed a petition to prohibit us from seeing Terri or, if that wasn't granted, to be allowed to severely restrict our visiting hours.

True or not, we felt that this was an act of retribution. The cruelty of it bewildered us. The Michael who had worked with me, sweated with me, and loved Terri with me, had disappeared. In his place was a man I prayed Terri had never seen.

His attack spurred us on. The husband of a teacher at Tampa Catholic advised us to contact a renowned lawyer named Joseph Magri, who, with his partner Robert Merkle, specialized in appeal

---

[2] I believe that God sends special people when you are in most need. For the next five years, Monsignor Malanowski had a tremendous influence on our lives. His strength and wisdom helped us maintain our sanity.

cases. He had known about our troubles and immediately agreed to represent us on a pro bono basis. Still, he'd need the transcript of the January 2000 trial, which would cost us in the neighborhood of $10,000 to obtain, money we didn't have. Magri, who looks like an elegant Paul Sorvino, impressed us from the start. Bob and I liked his honesty, his ability to tell us tough news gently but straightforwardly, his knowledge of the law, and his professionalism. For the first time, we felt we had a powerful ally. As he told us himself, the appeal process would be difficult. But at least it would be held in a different court with a different judge. We had a chance!

Meanwhile, as soon as Bobby told him of Greer's decision, Dave Pritchard, a teacher friend of Bobby's at Tampa Catholic, insisted we get a website going. He came up with Terrisfight.org, which it remains today. The site was used to get news of Terri's situation to anyone interested, and as it turned out, a lot of people were. The media did a story on the site; people began to email us with support and questions.

Another teacher, Frannie Siracusa, helped organize a celebrity charity basketball game at the high school to raise money for the appeal. The media publicized this as well. Star athletes from the Tampa Bay Buccaneers, Vinny Testaverde, of the New York Jets, and famous basketball and hockey players agreed to attend. I had no idea how many people would show up, let alone contribute, but to my surprise, there must have been six to eight hundred in the stands, a show of support that touched me profoundly. The support only escalated in the following years.

On March 24, 2000, Judge Greer imposed guidelines on the times we could visit Terri; insisted we draw up a "visitation guest list" for Michael's approval; authorized Michael to hire a security guard for Terri and one for himself; and granted Michael the right to pay these security costs out of Terri's medical fund.

Michael's excuse for needing the guards was that he'd observed some of Bobby's students praying for Terri's life outside the Palm Gardens nursing home. He described them as an "unruly mob," and said his and Terri's lives were in jeopardy. But Bobby's kids were well behaved, and they were just praying. They were as "dangerous" as pet kittens.

It seems that Greer was as aggravated as Michael that we had "dared" question his decision, and he gave us twenty minutes to come up with a list of people we would want to visit Terri.

"We couldn't think of anyone to put on the list," Suzanne remembers, "so we wrote down anybody and everybody we could think of—family, friends, who knows, just in case—so Terri would have visitors. And supporters."

One name was an inspiration of Bobby's: Frank Pavone. Unknown to Michael, Felos, or Judge Greer, Frank Pavone was a priest. Bobby had never met him, but he had heard him on television the night before, been impressed by his outspoken statements on pro-life issues, and figured he might, someday, come to our aid. Michael looked at our list and removed some names, but Frank Pavone, submitted without his priestly title, was not one of them. If he'd known the part Father Pavone would play later, his would have been one of the first names Michael crossed out.

On March 24, Judge Greer did issue a stay of the removal of the tube, to be in effect until all appellate remedies had been exhausted. Michael could sue to have his decision reversed, the judge said, but for whatever reason, Michael chose not to—at least not then.

He made a different move.

In early April, without consulting us or our attorney, Michael transferred Terri from the Palm Gardens nursing home to Woodside Hospice, a facility of the Hospice of the Florida Suncoast, in the city of Pinellas Park, just north of St. Petersburg. Again, this was supposedly for Terri's "protection." Michael needed a court order to have her transferred, and he got one without our knowledge. Who was chairman of the board of the hospice? George Felos.[3]

As soon as we found out about the transfer, Pam Campbell filed a motion with Judge Greer to have Terri transferred back to Palm Gardens. Since Terri had already moved, Greer said, the motion was irrelevant. Motion denied.

To me, putting Terri in a hospice was like putting her in jail. Michael was the jailer, Felos the warden. I could bang on the door, and they could let me in or not. I could scream for information, but they could ignore it. It was as though four hands were strangling me. Even as Terri continued to regress from lack of therapy and stimulation, evident in her clenched hands and by longer periods when it was difficult for her to respond, I felt she was being pushed further and further away. I imagined her crying out for her mother, and I was powerless to help her.

Bob and Bobby went to the hospice to speak to its administrator, Pat Sargent. They wanted to make sure Terri was getting the best care possible.

"We had one of the most heated arguments ever," Bobby reported.[4] We were very worried about Terri's safety and welfare

---

[3] Felos resigned his position in the same time frame Terri was transferred, but we have no doubt he still had influence.

[4] Sargent resigned from the hospice a few years later, though I'm not sure it had anything to do with the fight or with Terri.

because we knew she was now under Michael's complete control, and we could do nothing because of Felos's position on the board. We asked Pat Sargent if she'd let us know if Terri got sick. She stonewalled us. Well, then, we asked, what would she do if Terri got an infection? Her answer: Nothing.

"The argument started in the hall and continued into her office. She had to see we were very upset. Yes, she was in her legal right, but didn't she understand the human aspects? Eventually we backed off and calmed down, but I think I was almost as scared of my rage as Pat Sargent was. Even the hospice chaplain refused to help us. We turned to Joe Magri—and to the media.

"By this time, I was starting to have a little rapport with some of the reporters, and someone at Channel 28 put me on the air that night. I said, 'Hey, my sister's at a hospice now, and the hospice told me today that if Terri gets an infection, they won't tell my family and they'll let her die.'

"They had Felos on, too. 'That's hogwash,' he said. 'We'd never let her die.'"

Magri and Felos reached a compromise, though it wasn't easy. In early May, Michael verbally committed to the court words to the effect that Terri would get medical treatment at Woodside, thereby canceling a court hearing Magri had applied for.

Michael later reneged on the commitment. The following month, however, he signed a document worked out by Felos and Magri that stated the hospice would not terminate or withdraw Terri's treatment without prior notice to the court, and would treat Terri for five days if she got an infection. It meant that we would have a few days to fight if Terri got sick.

It's a testament to my state of mind that such small "victories"—things it seemed to me that any humane person could never dispute—gave me comfort.

Meanwhile, Magri, reflecting our concern that Michael and Felos were acting in concert to kill Terri, worked on the appeal of Greer's ruling removing the feeding tube. In early July, he filed with the appellate court to reverse the decision. His brief argued that the probate court had misapplied Florida law because it used an incorrect standard of proof; that Terri had a constitutional right to have all the evidence reviewed by a neutral arbiter; that Terri's First Amendment rights were violated; and that Terri's estate had been violated by wasting her money on legal fees.

Felos didn't file an "answer brief" with the appellate court until late August. His brief argued that the probate court ruling was correct and pleaded that Terri be allowed to die "naturally." I thought, *How can any sane human being consider starvation and dehydration "natural"?*

An oral hearing was scheduled for November 8. A three-member panel consisting of Judges Jerry Parker, Chris Altenbernd, and John Blue would preside at the appellate court in Lakeland.

Thus, some ten months after we had our emotional lives turned into chaos by Judge Greer, we would have to go through the same suspense, the same anxiety, the same uncertainty, all over again. With no guarantee that anything would be different at the end.

~~~⟋∾⟍~~~

Bobby's description of his life during those months applied
to us all:

"The case was starting to build some publicity, at least locally.
More and more people were learning about it, more and more
people became outraged. We were getting phone calls every day.
People were contacting the website, emailing us. Glenn Beck, who
at that time had a local radio show, was talking more about the case.
Every day our family would call each other—a dozen, two dozen
times—saying, 'Hey, is anything going on?' 'Have you heard from
any? …' 'Did we get any? …' 'Did Mr. Magri hear anything?' 'Any
good news from the lawyers?' Because I think each of us still had
the sense that truth would prevail. Something was going to happen
to stop this.

"Even when we were together on weekends or during the week,
as much as we were trying to make things feel normal, ultimately
all we could talk about was the case. Even during Christmas, even
when we *tried* to talk about things, it always came back to the case.
It obsessed our lives."

Chapter 10

Appeals

$\mathcal{B}$obby spoke to a friend of his who had worked with the appellate court for several years. He knew Judges Parker, Blue, and Altenbernd—particularly Altenbernd. The news wasn't good: Altenbernd was a liberal judge. Bobby's friend didn't think we had a chance.

"I was very concerned," Bobby says. "I conveyed what he had told me to my father, and we were all terribly worried. I felt we were blessed with Joseph Magri. When we first went to see him, his paralegals told us he had never lost a case. Besides, I thought his appellate brief was very strong, and so did friends of mine with lots more knowledge than I had."

I thought Magri made a brilliant case for us. But would a strong brief be enough? Bobby hadn't told me what he'd heard about Judge Altenbernd. He knew it would have made me nearly desperate with anxiety.

The oral hearing, it seemed to me, was our last chance. If the three judges turned down our appeal, Terri would die. It was this thought that made it so difficult for me to see her. Every time I entered her room, she would react. If I told her a joke or sang her a song, she would respond with a smile or a laugh. It was obvious to me—to all of us—that the noises she made, the movements toward us, her palpable joy in seeing us, were not involuntary reactions. And yet here were three men who had never seen her, never held her, never interacted with her, who would decide on our word or Michael's *depending on the quality of our testimony.*

Remember: Terri had been neglected since 1991—that's ten years! There was nothing in her files that indicated she was receiving proper therapy or rehabilitation.

Now, if you put a healthy person in bed for ten years and isolate them, they're going to deteriorate. Terri, in fact, was doing better than we might have expected. Warehoused, stimulated only when we were there, shown love or interest only from us, with us she was almost as reactive as she'd always been. I knew it was strength. I thought of it as courage. And I loved her all the more.

The appellate court's job was simply to rule on whether Judge Greer had followed the law. Magri could bring up some of the mistakes Greer had made, argue that he had followed the wrong law or depended on the wrong testimony—indeed, these he had covered in his brief. But the judges were only there to say, yes, he had followed the law, or no, he had not.

The format of the hearings was that each lawyer had fifteen minutes to testify, but the judges could interrupt at any time. The courtroom was small. I was struck by the fact that our side of the room was filled with about fifty supporters, while Michael's had only a few, including his father.

I felt good about the hearing. I was confident in Magri and excited that a person of his stature would go into that room to fight for us. But once the hearing started, I was the only optimistic member of my family.

Here's Bobby's take:

"I went to the appellate hearing, and my worst fears about Judge Altenbernd came true, because almost from the minute it started, he was all over Mr. Magri. His demeanor and his questions showed me where he stood on the issues, and I felt that Mr. Magri was on the defensive from the beginning, that he didn't have a chance to make his case. Altenbernd and I share the same gym in Tampa, and weeks later I saw him in the locker room, and I thought, *This scrawny little guy just decided my sister's fate.*"

Suzanne felt the same way Bobby did. "I was nervous to begin with," she says. "But once I started hearing Judge Altenbernd talk and the way he was treating Joe Magri and just the questions he was asking, I thought he was very negative. I felt then that the whole oral argument was negative. I mean, it was not a positive experience at all, and I couldn't say a word. None of us could. Altenbernd was really ruling the hearing. He hardly asked Felos any questions, and he made Magri defend himself with dozens of them."

And here's Bob:

"If I hadn't heard about Altenbernd from Bobby, I'd have thought we'd have a slam dunk, a no-brainer. Hearing about him, I was a little bit concerned, but not as concerned as I should have been. When I went into the actual hearing and I saw the way Altenbernd handled it, I thought, *This is done. It's over.* I knew immediately we were going to lose."

By the end of the hearing, I shared their mood. When we asked him for his impressions after the hearing ended, Magri, though still saying he was confident, admitted we had a problem.

Our last chance, it seemed, had failed.

On January 24, 2001, the Second District Court of Appeals ruled in favor of removing Terri's feeding tube. It felt as though the judges had taken up my battered heart and squeezed the life out of it.

The thing that galled me the most was that the judges described Michael as a loving, caring person who was trying to provide the best care for his wife. "It was like trying to make sense out of something that doesn't make sense," Bob recalled. "And your brain feels like it's going to explode."

I was at work the day the ruling came down. Bob called with the news and asked if I wanted him to come over. I was too numb to want support. "I'll be okay," I told him, knowing I wouldn't. "You call Bobby and Suzanne. They're a mess."

None of us was surprised by the ruling. "The first ruling with Greer," Bob says, "that one blew me away. I thought it was dishonest. The second one, I could tell the way Altenbernd handled it that he was going to rule against us. Then I was really worried. In talking with Magri before the ruling came in, I asked what our safety nets were. He said that of course we'd appeal the decision if it went against us, if necessary to the Florida Supreme Court and the United States Supreme Court. But he also said it was unlikely we'd get relief.

"And I knew personally I was preparing myself for what was coming. I was getting mentally conditioned for it, where I wasn't when Greer gave his ruling. At this juncture, I was preparing for it and trying to brace for the storm that was coming, because I knew it was going to happen."

I, too, braced myself. If the ruling goes against us, I vowed, we'd try and try and try again—whatever it took—to help Terri. But I had no idea what to do.

Desperation drove us forward. Bob stayed on the phones continuously, trying to win support for Terri from anyone who'd listen. He kept saying that something underhanded was going on, that at the very least we were seeing an old-boy network in operation.

We were boosted by an amazing call.

"Mr. Schindler?" a voice with a pronounced Texas drawl asked.

"Speaking."

"This is Ross Perot. I heard about your troubles, and I just want you to know that if you find a doctor to oversee Terri's rehabilitation, I'd like to help."

We were deeply moved. If so important a man knew about Terri, we figured, some of the publicity we were trying to generate had worked. And if he cared, others must care as well. We had been feeling lost, alone, defenseless against the power of the courts. Now a powerful voice spoke for our side.

Bob also got calls from police officers and retired sheriffs who told him we had obviously run into a heartless judge, but it was hardly much solace. Doctors and therapists called, offering their services for free. An organization involved with helping brain-injured individuals sent us letters from patients like Terri who had been misdiagnosed with PVS, evidence they felt we could use in our appeals.

Beginning in February and on through March 2001, the pace of court hearings became dizzying:

- Joe Magri files a motion for a rehearing by the appellate court, this time with all the appellate judges present. Denied.

- George Felos files to reverse Judge Greer's ruling prohibiting the removal of Terri's feeding tube until the entire appeals process is settled.

- Magri counterfiles, asking the appellate court for a thirty-day stay of the removal. Granted. Greer orders the tube removed once the appellate court's stay is over. Magri files with the appellate court for an extension of the stay until an appeal before the Florida Supreme Court is heard. He is told to file with the Supreme Court, and that no stay beyond that filing date would be granted.

The prevailing trend was easy to see: Terri's chances were growing dim. The day of her death could not be far away.

Suzanne asked her divorce lawyer, Jane Grossman,[1] **to** recommend someone to take on perjury charges against Michael, a case Magri said he was ill equipped to handle. "Well," Jane replied, "there's this high-profile attorney who's got a great reputation. Her name's Pat Anderson." Bob and Bobby went to see her.

"We spent several hours just talking to her and her partner, Jim Eckert," Bob remembers. "They immediately recognized what was going on. Eckert jumped to his feet. 'This means war!' he shouted, pounding on the table. 'It's outrageous. Let's go get 'em.'"

On April 12, 2001, Pat filed in the circuit court to disqualify Judge Greer from Terri's case due to discrepancies in the trial. Four days later, Greer denied the motion. (How Greer could decide on

---

1   Suzanne had been divorced from her first husband for several years.

his own competence mystified me then and baffles me now.) On April 18, the Florida Supreme Court refused to hear Terri's case and refused to extend Terri's stay beyond 1 p.m. on April 20. Anderson immediately filed a petition asking the federal court to intervene, arguing that Terri's civil rights were being violated.

On April 20, the federal court conducted a morning hearing. "I thought Pat did well," Bobby told us after it ended. "The judge— he was an old-time judge—had a good reputation. My impression was that he didn't want to go anywhere near the case. Like he didn't want to have anything to do with it and was trying to find some way out. And he found a way."

That afternoon, the judge ruled that Terri's case was a matter for the country's highest court and extended Terri's stay to 5:00 p.m. on April 23, 2001, so we could lodge an appeal with the U.S. Supreme Court itself.

I get confused writing about these hearings and counterhearings, even with my notes in front of me and in the calm of retrospect. Imagine trying to keep up with the frantic pace of events when I was so frantic myself I could barely eat, sleep, or think. For the most part, Magri's and Anderson's maneuvers were beyond me, and I took no comfort in their words of reassurance: "This time we have a good chance." I felt I was being tossed like a giant beach ball from stranger's hand to stranger's hand, helpless over where I landed. I remember little detail about those days, only the sense of floating from hour to hour without strength, without control, without comprehension.

I went to see Terri every day, pretending cheerfulness, acting as though nothing momentous was happening, singing and joking as always, but with a hollowness in my heart that I prayed she would not detect. And Terri would smile when I entered and protest when I left by trying to hold on to me, her sweetness undiminished.

On April 23, 2001, Justice Anthony Kennedy of the U.S. Supreme Court refused to hear Terri's case.

On April 24, 2001, Terri's feeding tube was removed, and she was left to die.

Chapter 11
Reprieve

"Prepare yourself for Terri's death," Joe Magri told us. "Start making funeral arrangements." Our family had different reactions to his words.

"I had despaired," Bobby says. "It was done. We were done. There was no hope."

"I was just numb," Suzanne adds. "I just remember walking out of the hospice in a daze—maybe I was in shock. I don't remember thinking, *Well, this is over and done with. There's nothing left to say and nothing left to do,* but I do remember feeling, *This can't be happening.*"

"What I was doing," Bob says, "was trying to tell everyone, including myself, that it's over. That we'd lost—there was nothing more we could do, we'd tried everything—and God rest Terri's soul."

I was the only one who refused to accept the inevitable. *The Lord's not going to let her die like that. She's not going to starve to death*

Terri's feeding tube was removed. The event received only minimal attention. Glenn Beck, the local radio host, reported on her condition from the hospice grounds. Some thirty people prayed outside the hospice. Police guarded Terri's door.

Bob asked the hospice administrator, Mary Labyak, to make sure Terri got her palliative care—something as simple as ice chips, for example—and Labyak assured him she would. Later that day, Bobby visited Terri and found that no care was being given. He called Labyak in a fury. "What about the care Terri was promised?" he asked. Labyak said Terri wasn't to be given any. "Then you basically lied to my father and you lied to our attorney," Bobby shouted, and slammed down the phone.

Soon afterward, one of our friends, Jana Carpenter, took Suzanne aside. A nurse herself, she was angry at the lack of care Terri was receiving, so mad that the two women drove to police headquarters to lodge a complaint. The police wouldn't listen.

"We're buying baby food," Jana told Suzanne. "You're gonna go in there and feed that girl." Greer's order did not say anything about denying her food by mouth.

Suzanne remembers the incident clearly. "We bought two jars of baby food and went back to the hospice. Jana wasn't on the visitors' list, so I went into Terri's room alone while Bobby stayed outside, talking to one of the administrators. There was another nurse in the room. 'What do you have in your hand?' she asked.

"'Baby food. Would you please feed it to her?'

"'*Feed* her? We can't do that.'

"'You're not giving her care. I'm definitely going to try to feed her.'

"Well, they all came rushing in—the head nurse and two other nurses—and marched me outside. I told them I was sorry and asked again if I could feed Terri. 'Absolutely not!' they said. 'If you feed her she might choke.'

"I mean, give me a break! They tell me she might choke, which doesn't make a lot of sense, since she's dying anyway. I'm afraid I blew up. I got in the head nurse's face. 'Would you starve your pet to death? How would you feel about that?' I yelled. 'You're starving a girl to death. How do you feel about *that*? You're a mother. From one mother to another, I hope you can't sleep at night.'

"The police made us leave the building. Someone told Michael about the incident, and Bobby and I were banned from going to the hospice again, which meant that if Terri died then, we wouldn't be allowed to be with her."[1]

The following day, I decided to take some of Terri's stuff home—make-work so I didn't have to think of the future. On the way home, we all stopped at the McDonald's around the corner. Bob and Bobby went inside to order a cup of coffee; Suzanne and I stayed in the parking lot.

Bob's cell phone rang. The call was from Chris O'Connell, a reporter from Bay News 9, the local cable station in the Tampa Bay area. The family, and Bobby in particular, had built up a good relationship with Chris. He had a cousin in a similar condition as Terri's, so he could probably empathize—at any rate, he was always nice to us, and we liked him.

He asked Bob if we'd come down to do an interview. But I didn't want to go. I just did not want to go. My daughter's feeding

---

[1]   We had to go in front of Judge Greer to rescind the ban, one of his few rulings in our favor. Bobby and Suzanne were allowed back into the hospice six months later, in October.

tube had just been removed, and I was in no condition to do anything. I wanted to be home. That was my only wish: to be home.

"We were out in the parking lot," Bobby remembers. I said to my dad, 'You know, Chris has been pretty good to us. Maybe you can appeal to the public for help. The station's on the way home. Why don't we stop and give him a quick interview?'

"Dad agreed. He said, 'Okay, we'll stop for Chris.'

"And that was the biggest decision ever made in the case."

Bobby continues:

"Dad was interviewed outside the station by Chris. Mom and Suzy waited with me in the parking lot. I got out of the car. A man named Tim Boyle, a senior producer at the station, came up to me.

"'It's funny meeting you here,' he said. 'I was thinking about you.'

"We only knew each other casually. 'Why?'

"'I was riding my bike last night with my headphones on, and I was listening to an interview with Michael Schiavo's ex-girlfriend. Did you hear the interview?'

"'No. You mean Cindy Shook?'

"'I think that's her name. You might want to listen to what she said. She said some pretty mean things about Michael.'

"Wow! We'd been trying to locate Cindy, but she'd broken up with Michael years ago, and we didn't know how to find her. She no longer had her job as a nurse at the hospital where Michael later got a job.

"Dad had finished his interview. I brought Tim over. 'It may be in your best interests to locate this girl,' he told dad after he'd repeated his story.

"'Maybe we should tell this to Joe Magri,' Dad said. 'Run it by him and see what he has to say.'

"Lawyers are funny. Some things you tell them that you think are really important, they blow it off. But when I called Joe, I thought he was going to come right through the phone. 'You need to find that girl and find out exactly what she said,' he shouted. *'Now!'* Over the years, the courts had believed that Michael was the 'good guy.' If we had a witness who refuted his story that Terri had expressed a wish to die, surely they would hear our case with more sympathy.

"I called the station. The DJ who interviewed Cindy was a woman named Carrie Kirkland, and she confirmed everything Tim had told me. Yes, the woman was Cindy Shook. Yes, Ms. Shook had said Michael was not the type of person everybody thought he was. He was abusive. He had a violent temper. He had stalked her after they broke up, years ago. He once tried to drive her off the road. Amazing stuff! She was afraid of him even now, she said, all these years later. She was now married with young children and didn't want him to jeopardize them. She was only moved to call the station because she had heard Michael bad-mouthing our family on a local morning show, and she couldn't let it go. She had to tell listeners what kind of a man he was."

I had mixed feelings when Bobby reported all this to me. Maybe Magri was right: maybe the information could help Terri. But maybe we would have our hopes raised only to have them dashed again. I was so exhausted that Cindy's explosive news didn't excite me the way it excited Bob and Bobby. They had heard the tone of Magri's voice. Michael was an abuser! A stalker! He might have abused Terri! The judge would have to believe us now!

Bobby again:

"I have a very close friend, Eddie Cotilla, who works for an investigative firm. I got a copy of the Cindy tape and immediately called Eddie and asked him to track Cindy down.

"It wasn't difficult. Cindy lived in Brandon[2] under her married name, Brasher, and Eddie located her within hours. 'I called her, but couldn't get anywhere with her. She was too scared of Michael. So I said, 'Dad, you call her.'"

Bob did: "I had no more success than Bobby," he reported. "Cindy repeated her accusations about Michael's abusiveness, but that was all. 'I will not go public,' she said right away. 'And if you try to subpoena me, I'll forget everything I just told you.' Those were her exact words.

"I called Joe Magri and told him everything that Cindy Shook had said. 'Can we keep her anonymous?' I asked Joe. 'Otherwise she won't talk.'

"'Impossible,' he answered. 'We'll do everything we can to protect her, but you've got to be honest with her and say her name's going to come out if it's used in court.'

"I called Cindy back and pleaded with her to go public with her statement. 'You're a parent now,' I told her. 'If it was one of your children ... what they're doing to Terri, they're killing her right now! Please, please come out.'

"She still refused: 'No. My children. I'm afraid he'll kill my children.'"

---

[2] About twenty-five miles east of St. Petersburg.

When Bob told me about the call, I was overwhelmed. I knew Michael could become enraged—I had seen plenty of that!—but Cindy's fear was beyond anything I could have imagined. I sympathized with her, absolutely understood her desire not to testify. But Terri's life was a stake. She had already gone a day and a half without food. And there was no chance the tube would be reinserted if Cindy didn't speak out.

Bob called our other lawyer, Pat Anderson, and asked her to help. She and her partner, Jim Eckert, dispatched an investigator, Kim Takacs, to Cindy's house.

"For some reason, Cindy spoke to her," Bobby says. "She said a lot of things to Kim that she said to my father and me. And Kim wrote it all down so that it could be used in an affidavit. Pat and Jim took the evidence to Judge Greer and filed for an emergency injunction based on Cindy's evidence."

In taking her deposition, Jim Eckert played the audiotape of Cindy's conversation with the DJ. She was describing the time when her feelings toward Michael changed:

Cindy: I'm sort of personal with the case because I was the first girl that Michael Schiavo dated after his wife had this heart attack. It was about three years after she had her heart attack.

DJ: Right.

Cindy: And he used to go visit her at the nursing home while we were dating. … It was before he ever filed his lawsuit … He's a real loud guy, and he would go through the nursing home. And he said immediately as soon as he got near the door, her head was already looking at the door because she would recognize his voice.

DJ: Right

Cindy: And she would start crying when he got ready to leave. And he was like, "She has ruined years of my life, and she has taken all this time—and obsessed my whole life with this, and this is all her fault"—just a complete change.

DJ: Really?

Cindy: ... "I was just like, I don't even know who you are, but just get away from me and—

DJ: How long did you date him?

Cindy: I dated him for a year.

DJ: I talked to somebody else who knows the family personally ... and they said there was a little bit of an emotional abusive relationship going on with them. Do you know anything about that?

Cindy: I don't know from him, but she was kind of heavy as a child, and—

DJ: And he would call her fat, and that's why she was so anorexic and bulimic. Right?

Cindy: [He said] she was bulimic, and there's no way somebody could be taking all those laxatives ... Mike's very possessive; he's very jealous. He stalked me at my—at where I worked after I stopped dating.[3] When he would get mad at me he would tell me, "I would rather be with her laying in that bed in the nursing home than you." I mean, he can be the most incredibly mean person.

DJ: What a nice guy ...

---

[3] Under Felos's questioning, Cindy agreed that Michael might not have been stalking her at the hospital where she worked—he had gotten a job at the same hospital— but that he would follow her in his car when she drove, and that throughout 1993, there were often twelve to fifteen phone calls a day that nobody answered when she picked up. She was sure they were from Michael. On redirect, she said that when she found out that Michael had gotten a job at the hospital and was looking for her, she was shocked and scared.

During her deposition, Jim Eckert followed up on Cindy's statement that she was scared when Michael got a job at the hospital.

Q: (Jim Eckert): If you were afraid of him, did you report this to management?

A: (Cindy Shook): Yes.

Q: And what was the reaction of management?

A: That unless I had a restraining order there was nothing they could do.

Q: Did you ever attempt to get a restraining order?

A: No.

Q: Did you ever think about getting a restraining order?

A: Yes.

Q: When was that?

A: During that time.

Q: Was it during the same time he was following you also?

A: Yes ...

Q: Did you ever talk to anybody about getting a restraining order?

A: Yes ... An off-duty police officer ... May have been a deputy sheriff.

Jim Eckert asked her about Terri's wishes as well.

Q: Did you ever have a conversation with him about what he and she had discussed about living or dying in the event they had a stroke or automobile accident or anything else like that?

A: No ...

Q: How long were you and he friends?

A: I think about ten months.

Q: How often would you see him during that time period?

A: Every few days; every two or three days.

Q: What would you do?

A: We had an anatomy class together. We just hung out a lot at one or the other of our residences and talked.

Q: So you must have had lots of conversations then. Right?

A: Yes.

Q: And did he discuss Terri with you?

A: Yes … He talked about her medical care; he talked about different options of things he could do to make sure she was cared for in the best possible way.

Q: Did he want her to live?

A: I don't know.

Q: Did he ever say he wanted her to die?

A: No.

Q: Did he ever indicate to you that she had indicated that she wanted to die?

A: No.

And, when Eckert asked her about her statement to Kim Takacs, this:

Q: Now it goes on to say … that Mr. Schiavo became angry when you asked him questions about Terri Schiavo.

A: Yes …

Q: It goes on to give a quote there, "How the hell should I know—we never spoke about this, my God, I'm only twenty-five years old." Did you say that? …

A: What he said to me is "How the hell should I know. We were young. We never spoke of this."

Q: What was "this"?

A: What to do with her now. The only conversations I had with him were related to what to do with her now … How he could get on with his life … He and I had many discussions about the fact that he felt like he wanted to get on with his life, and he talked about the option ... about building an addition to her parents' home. He talked about other options ...

Q: What were the other options you talked about?

A: Hire private staff in the nursing home she was in to be there twenty-four hours a day, move her to another nursing home and hire staff to be with her twenty-four hours a day.

Q: Anything else?

A: No.

Q: Was there ever any discussion of conversations he had with her about her wishing to die in the event of an incident such as what happened to her? ...

A: No.

Q: Did he ever indicate to you that she and he had had discussions about wanting not to live in the event of an incident such as what happened to her?

A: No.

"Terri's feeding tube had been removed now for over two days," Bobby went on. "But Judge Greer refused to issue an injunction because it was thirteen months after the original trial started. The statute of limitations, he ruled, said that new evidence had to be submitted within a year.

"So on April 26, Anderson and Eckert made a brilliant move. They filed an action against Michael in civil court, taking it out of the probate division where Greer presided. They went before a new judge, Frank Quesada, who agreed to an emergency hearing that evening.

"All of us were at the house that night, including my ex-girlfriend and my niece, Alexandra, and we were on pins and needles, waiting to hear how Quesada was going to rule."

The phone rang. Bob picked it up. I couldn't hear what he was saying—he had his back turned to us—but when he hung up and looked at me, there was an expression on his face I've never seen before or since, and now that Terri's dead, will never see again. His eyes shone; he was smiling; his facial muscles worked to control emotions that seemed to want to burst from him. "That was a reporter from the *Tampa Tribune*," he said. "He just walked out of the courtroom. The hearing's still going on, but he said"—his voice broke—"he said it looks like Judge Quesada is going to issue an injunction. He'll call us back."

I stopped breathing. My heart was pounding so furiously I thought my chest would explode. We had the television set on, Bay News 9, and Chris O'Connell broke in from the steps of courthouse and said that Judge Quesada had just issued a temporary injunction. He ordered that Terri's tube be reinserted.

We all started jumping around, cheering and hugging each other and crying for joy. Little Alex, then seven, ran to the bathroom and got a box of Kleenex, which she passed around to everyone. And then everybody went down on their hands and knees, and we said a prayer and we thanked God.

I didn't quite believe what we had just heard, but for some reason, in my heart, I wasn't surprised. I'd felt something good would happen, and it did.

I never thought Terri's rescue that night was a miracle. Her life was spared because Cindy Shook was courageous enough to talk, because Pat Anderson and Jim Eckert understood the legal maneuvering necessary to get the case, at least temporarily, out of Greer's hands, and because a wise and humane judge felt there was an argument to be made for Terri's salvation. But as we knelt in our living room, we were all aware of the presence of God.

Bobby, who until Terri was saved was perhaps the most doubting of us, tells of a strange experience:

"A couple of days before Terri's feeding tube was removed, someone at the school where I taught handed me a prayer card with Padre Pio's picture on it to take in to pray with Terri.[4] And the day Terri's feeding tube was removed, a young boy I didn't know gave me medals of Padre Pio. They were nice gestures, but I thought little of them.

"So here's what was really strange. Right after Terri's feeding tube was reinserted, I went down to Pat Anderson's office—she had become our lead attorney and coincidentally had moved into a new office. I walked in the door and there on the bookshelf was a picture of Padre Pio—a huge picture. And I said, 'Pat, who gave you that?'

"'Oh,' she goes—and Pat is not of our faith—'nobody. That picture was here when I moved in. I don't even know who it is.'

"It was one of those coincidences, you know, that makes you think for a moment."

---

4 Padre Pio wasn't a saint then. He has since been canonized.

Chapter 12

Reality Returns

I want to say this clearly for the record: Bob and I were willing—no, eager—to pay for Terri's care; it would have cost Michael nothing, not even the money left in Terri's medical fund. We could have offered her at-home private nursing through contributions, which were beginning to come in regularly on our website, supplemented by Bob's and my earnings.

In the two years following Terri's collapse, we probably could have negotiated a monetary agreement with Michael regarding Terri's care. Even right after he won his malpractice lawsuit, we might have been able to compromise. But we were friends, and negotiations seemed unnecessary, so the matter didn't come up.

By 2001, compromise was impossible. Terri would live or Terri would die. Those were the stakes.

And the battle raged on.

Judge Quesada had issued only a temporary injunction prohibiting the removal of Terri's feeding tube.[1] Our job now was to make sure it was permanent. We needed fresh evidence beyond

---

[1] Felos immediately filed suit to have it overturned. He was denied.

Cindy's affidavit, and if we couldn't produce it, Judge Greer's February 11, 2000, death order would stand.

On the eve of Terri's 2000 trial, while she was still in the Palm Gardens nursing home, Suzanne's husband, Michael Vitadamo, brought a video camera into Terri's room and made a tape of her moving, responding, interacting with her family. The tape was grainy, dark, and indistinct, but you didn't have to be an expert on PVS to see that Terri was cognizant. It was presented to Judge Greer. Greer disagreed with the evidence.

Nevertheless, when shown on television, it was seen by the neurologist Dr. William Hammesfahr, a Nobel Prize nominee for his discovery of a revolutionary type of therapy for stroke victims.

Dr. Hammesfahr contacted Pat Anderson and submitted an affidavit saying categorically that Terri was not PVS (despite a decade of no rehabilitation). Furthermore, he asked Michael's permission to begin the first phase of his recovery program on Terri. Five other doctors submitted similar affidavits, and Pat presented them all to Judge Greer.

Once again, Judge Greer denied Pat's request to overturn his ruling that Terri's feeding tube be removed, and once again Pat turned to the court of appeals, claiming that Greer had not taken into account the "new evidence"—Cindy's deposition and the affidavits of the six physicians. The appellate court ordered oral arguments to be heard on June 25,[2] again before the panel of Judges Parker, Blue, and Altenbernd.

---

[2] Meanwhile, on April 26, Pat filed a complaint in civil court accusing Michael of fraud and perjury. On May 6, she amended the complaint to include breach of fiduciary duty and conspiracy, among other charges. On June 14, Felos gave notice that Michael would not be available for his scheduled deposition. On two separate occasions, subpoena servers could not locate Michael. His and his fiancée's whereabouts were unknown. The deposition was rescheduled four or five times. Michael didn't appear for any of them. No penalty was leveled against him. Eventually, the civil suit was thrown out.

On July 11, the appellate court ruled that Pat could file a motion before Judge Greer requesting "evidentiary hearings." On July 23, Felos struck back by requesting Judge Greer to issue an order immediately discontinuing Terri's feeding tube even before he reviewed any of the evidence Pat had submitted. Greer turned down the request, though he did authorize a payment of $54,900 to Felos from Terri's medical fund, bringing the total taken from the fund to some $300,000.

By this time, Judge Quesada had been transferred to family court, and the chief judge of the Sixth Circuit, David A. Demers, while keeping the suit against Michael for fraud in civil court, ruled that all matters having to do with Terri's life or death be settled in Judge Greer's court. If Greer ruled against Terri, it seemed, we would have no place to go. And my hope, which had begun to flower, died.

On August 7, 2001, Greer once again ordered Terri's tube removed, and set August 28 as the date. He admitted he had not read the six doctors' affidavits.

One of us—Bob, Suzanne, Bobby, or I—was in one court or another throughout the summer. Occasionally we heard good news: were Michael ever brought up on perjury and fraud charges in civil court, we believed we would be able to negotiate a settlement with him, freeing him from paying damages and freeing Terri into our care. More often the news squelched our hopes. Greer turned down motion after motion.[3] We could see our attorneys' frustration, and it only increased our own.

---

[3] In August 2001, for example, Pat filed a "motion of bias" requesting Greer to remove himself from the case because his eyesight was so bad he could not see Terri's reactions in the videotape. Greer turned down the motion.

We united as a family; I think that saved us from breaking down psychologically. Otherwise, the tension would have driven us mad. I've seen families torn apart under daily stress. Our bonds grew stronger.

Greer's admission that he had not read the doctors' affidavits gave Pat ammunition. At an August 16 news conference, she announced she would seek federal protection for Terri under the Americans with Disabilities Act. Terri's civil rights as a mentally and physically disabled person were being violated, Pat claimed.

Evidently unwilling to have the federal court intervene, Greer granted Terri a stay of execution until October 9 to allow Terri "due process of law" in the court of appeals.[4] And the appellate court called for yet another round of oral arguments, based on the doctors' affidavits. On the basis of those hearings, they ordered that five doctors—two from Terri's side, two from Michael's, and one appointed by the court—examine Terri to determine whether she could improve. Essentially, it meant a new trial—again to be conducted by Judge Greer—at a date to be determined.

"I was in Pat's office when the order came in," Bobby remembers. "It was another decision that again was either potentially going to save Terri's life or mean the end of her life, and I was as nervous as I was when we waited for Judge Greer's original decision, so when they ruled for us, it was huge. *Huge!*

"It was an ecstatic moment. I think Pat, too, felt that we had turned a corner. She was overflowing with joy. We were all very, very happy that day. It was the happiest I'd been in a long time."

---

4 He had also ruled, in a different appeal, that Bobby and Suzanne could once again be admitted to see Terri, provided they made no effort to feed her. But terms were strict: no pictures could be distributed to our doctors to assist them in their evaluation of Terri's condition, and Michael would have exclusive rights to any videotapes or still photographs of Terri.

I shared Bobby's happiness. This was the first time that the three-judge panel had ruled in our favor. The doctors' examination, whether they were our doctors, Michael's, or the court's, would surely see what I saw: A girl responding. A girl aware.

Naturally Felos sued to have the appellate court decision overturned. He was turned down. In November 2001, Greer held a "case management" hearing to establish procedures and time frames for Terri to be examined by the five doctors. When in December Felos, perhaps nervous about the outcome of the hearing, suggested an unbinding mediation between the two sides, Greer agreed to appoint a mediator—Horace Andrews, a retired judge.

I had doubts about mediation, but Bob and I agreed to go along with it. Maybe, just maybe, Michael would come to his senses, and we would be able to offer him enough in terms of money and peace of mind to let us have Terri back.

Two ground rules were established for the mediation: Bobby and Suzanne would not attend, just Michael, Bob, and me, and our respective lawyers. And neither we nor Michael were to disclose to anyone what was said between us.

We met in a room in the courthouse. Michael was hostile from the start. "Who are you?" he shouted at attorney Celia Bachman, Pat's associate. "What are you doing here?"

Judge Andrews tried to calm him down, and suggested that he and Bob meet in a private room with no lawyers present. "I think that Mr. Schindler and Mr. Schiavo should try to discuss their differences," he said. "I'll sit between them and maybe they can settle this."

Michael and Bob in a room together with only an eighty-seven-year-old judge between them? They'd kill each other, and the judge, I thought. "Absolutely not," I said. "I'll go in Bob's place."

"Is that all right with you, Mr. Schiavo?" Judge Andrews asked.

Michael shrugged. "Sure."

I knew I could never negotiate an agreement between Michael and us; the lawyers could do that later. But maybe if we agreed on some small things, it would be a start. The atmosphere in the courtroom was so antagonistic that I'm sure all Judge Andrews wanted to do was to find some common ground on some issues. Anything.

When the three of us sat down, Michael kept his head averted, but I looked straight at him, feeling calm and in control. I tried to recall the time I thought of him as Terri's husband and my ally—the good Michael, not the rage-filled man beside me.

This is how I remember the session going.

"Do you have anything to say, Mrs. Schindler," the judge asked quietly.

"Three things," I answered. "I'd like to get Terri's wheelchair fixed. I'd like to be able to take her outside. And I'd like her to get rehabilitation."

Judge Andrews turned to Michael. "Is that all right with you, Mr. Schiavo?"

Michael looked at me. All I could see in his eyes was fury. "Why do you want to get her wheelchair fixed?"

"Michael," I said patiently. "She can't go out. She can't go anywhere."

"You can put her in the Geri chair[5] and take her out."

"It's too unwieldy to take her to the mall. That's where she loved to go when she lived with us. Remember, Michael?"

"The mall? You can't take her there, anyway."

I fought my own anger and switched gears. "You promised you'd get her rehabilitation. You've broken your promise."

"She already had two years of rehab, and it's not going to help her."

"Michael, those were the first two years," I said. "She hasn't had any rehab for nine years."

He glared at me. "She's beyond help."

I stayed steely calm. "I want to take her outside."

"You can."

"No, we're never *allowed* to take her outside."

He stood up suddenly. I thought he was going to attack. "Mr. Schiavo, I think you had better sit down," Judge Andrews said.

He remained standing. "What about your son and daughter?"

"What does that mean?" I asked, bewildered. "Taking her outside has nothing to do with my son and daughter."

"They never go see her. They never—" He stopped, perhaps remembering that for many months they were not allowed in the hospice. "Now all of a sudden Bobby's the spokesperson for Terri Schiavo on television and all over, in the newspapers. Bobby this, Bobby that."

---

[5] Kind of a recliner on wheels.

Terri, one year old, in her
first professional photo

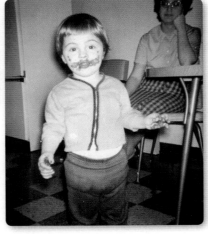

Terri in a fight with
chocolate frosting

Terri loving her brother Bobby,
only 13 months younger

Terri and Bobby with
their Uncle Mikey

Our family at Uncle Mikey's wedding, 1969

Christmas day, 1969: Bobby, Suzanne, and Terri

A visit with Santa

Suzanne, Bobby, and Terri—happy times

The kids with Mema and Pepa
in Corning, New York

Terri's girlfriend, Sue Kolb,
Suzanne, and Terri on Halloween

Terri's first Holy Communion:
Bobby, Suzanne, Bob's mom, and
Bob's Aunt Anna

The Three Musketeers

Terri's never-before-seen artwork

WOLVES

Senior year, 1981, at Archbishop Wood High School

Terri's first ski trip in high school, with girlfriends Sue and Sara

Bobby at graduation from La Salle University, 1987, with Suzanne and Terri

Terri's wedding, 1984

Terri's family wedding photo, 1984

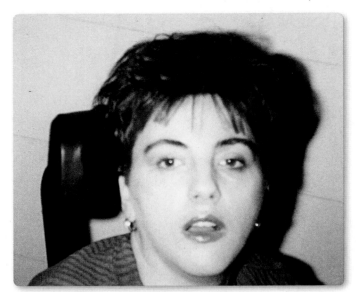

Terri, after getting her hair done

At the mall, before Terri's therapy was withheld

He kept going on at me, repeating Bobby's and Suzanne's names. I didn't understand what he was trying to say.

Judge Andrews did his best. "Mr. Schiavo, you've got to sit down. If we don't talk about this quietly and calmly, we're not going to get anything settled."

"We're not going to get anything settled, anyway," Michael said, and stormed out of the room.

Judge Andrews and I sat staring at the door, saying nothing. Soon I got up, gathered Bob, Pat, and Celia, and left the courthouse. Although the mediation was supposed to be kept secret, the media were there and Felos was talking to them. I don't remember what he said—probably that Michael was trying to come to an amicable agreement and we were stopping him. "I can't believe what he's doing," Pat said to Judge Andrews. "He's violating already!" Andrews just walked away.

Later, under the terms of the mediation agreement, I would write my version of the meeting, and Michael his. But nothing ever came of our statements, and looking at mine now, I remember how futile the day was. I felt sick. Mute. Hollow.

Abused.

Chapter 13

The Doctors' Trial

*S*ummers were always our favorite times. The children were home from school, we went to Corning or to the Jersey Shore, all of us had time to play. But the summer of 2002—like the ones immediately before and the ones to come—was filled with legal maneuvering, heated conversations with our lawyers, and worry and fear. Bob reminded me recently that we hadn't had a vacation of more than a few days since Terri collapsed. Every weekend we reserved a day to visit Terri, and before my mother passed away, we would visit them both. Bob says Mother's Day was especially hard for him. "When most mothers were going to a brunch or dinner, Mary's Mother's Day was in a nursing home. But she never complained because that's where she wanted to be."

Still, by 2002, the daily pressure was almost too much to bear.

October 11, 2002, was the date set by Judge Greer for doctors to begin their testimony. It was nearly one year after the appellate court set a mandatory hearing on Terri's medical condition. Essentially it was a trial to determine whether Terri was in a persistent vegetative state, not to determine what her wishes would be if she were ever in that state. I looked forward to it because I was sure it would prove that Terri was not PVS, and also because it might explain the reason for her collapse.

By now, Bob and I were positive that our healthy, blooming daughter had had neither bulimia nor a heart attack. Without our knowledge, several of our supporters petitioned the Department of Children and Families to investigate what she *had* suffered from, and the DCF assigned an investigator to the task. His report—kept confidential under DCF rules—was never revealed. When Pat Anderson subpoenaed him to appear in court and reveal his findings, Judge Greer stopped it cold.[1]

Bob and I both believed that Michael had done something bad to Terri the night she collapsed, but we had no evidence. We didn't suspect he had planned to harm her but had hurt her in one of his rages, causing her to fall. The lapse between the time Michael said Terri collapsed (somewhere between 4:30 and 5:00 a.m.) and time the paramedics arrived (at 5:52, approximately six minutes after the 911 call, according to their log) leaves at the very least more than fifty minutes unaccounted for. We wonder what Michael was doing in that period. Trying to revive Terri by himself? Panicking because he had fought with his wife and she had collapsed? We don't know, and will probably never know. We *do* know that Michael gave different versions of what happened that night, and this deepened our suspicions. If he had called 911 immediately, as he claims, why did Bob have to tell him to do it, and why was it almost an hour before the paramedics arrived?

The legal maneuvering continued. Pat petitioned Greer for another guardianship hearing attempting to remove Michael as

---

[1] To this day, we don't know what it said.

guardian; Greer upheld Michael when he moved to prevent the hearing. Michael filed with the Florida Supreme Court to overturn the appellate court's ruling requiring medical testing; the supreme court denied his motion. Our doctors produced a list of medical and neurological tests they wanted Terri to undergo; Judge Greer approved three of them, denied a dozen others. Judge Greer approved payment for Michael's appointed doctors, but denied payment for ours.

On October 2, 2002, nine days before the trial was to begin, Michael petitioned the court to authorize Terri's "cremation upon her death." Greer approved the petition.

I remember Bobby's outrage. "It's against our faith," he cried. "And against Terri's faith, and Michael knows that."

Did he do it out of spite? we all wondered. And Bobby, in his misery, asked, "Or did he want to hide something he may have done to Terri the night she collapsed—something only flames could hide?"

His question remains unanswered.[2]

Meanwhile, Felos mounted a campaign against Dr. Hammesfahr, the Nobel-candidate neurologist who was the first medical authority to say that Terri was not in a persistent vegetative state. Felos pointed out that Hammesfahr's name was included on a website listing incompetent doctors, calling him "Dr. Quack."

---

[2] In his 2005 book, *Silent Witness: The Untold Story of Terri Schiavo's Death,* author Mark Fuhrman lists six possible scenarios of Terri's collapse, one of which is that Michael and Terri struggled the night of February 25 and that he unwittingly got her in a choke hold, cutting off oxygen to her brain, which, at that time, could not have been visually detected or later revealed in Terri's autopsy.

"It was terrible," Bob says. "I had been to Hammesfahr's office, and I'd seen some of the astonishing work he'd done with stroke patients. And here Felos is painting him like he's insane. Dr. Hammesfahr has contributed more to humanity than most doctors could ever dream of doing."

Nevertheless, we had faith that Judge Greer would see through Felos's tactics.

The medical examinations were held over the summer prior to the October trial. Dr. Hammesfahr was one of our examining physicians, Dr. William Maxfield—chosen by Pat—the other. Michael's doctors conducted the first examinations. One of them, Dr. Melvin Greer (no relation to the judge), spent at best twenty to thirty minutes with Terri. The other, Dr. Ronald Cranford, a right-to-die activist who calls himself "Dr. Humane Death," spent an hour with her, examining and videotaping her.

During his examination, Dr. Cranford asked her to look at a balloon and to follow it with her eyes. "Good, Terri," he said. "You see the balloon. You're doing it. Good job." He asked her to do other simple tasks, and each time complimented her. "Great, Terri. You hear what I'm saying. You're following my orders."

We knew what she was capable of, for we had witnessed it many times before, but it thrilled me to see her react so clearly to a "hostile" doctor.

Judge Greer's choice of doctor—the man ostensibly without bias, beholden to neither side—was Dr. Peter Bambakidis, who was to arrive in Tampa the same day Michael's doctors examined Terri. He was supposed to get to the hospice somewhere around 4:00 p.m.

Bob and I waited for him in Terri's room. Felos and Michael were in the waiting room, stone-faced and silent. We must have waited an hour for Bambakidis to show, and when he didn't, we went to the waiting room. Michael and Felos had left, so we went home. Perhaps Bambakidis would appear the next day.

"What happened," Bob remembers with outrage, "was that Felos went to the airport to pick up Bambakidis and bring him to the hospital later that night, once we'd left and without our knowing about it. *Felos! Picking up the neutral doctor!*

"Michael said that he had arrived back at the hospice around 6:30 that evening, and that Bambakidis had arrived to observe Terri. Not only did they not videotape the session, but none of our family was there to see it. We had only the word of Felos and Michael that Bambakidis actually examined Terri."

By contrast, Hammesfahr's examination, witnessed by all, was thorough—and thrilling. Suzanne describes the session best:

"Hammesfahr spent the better part of three hours with Terri and videotaped it all. At first, he worked on Terri's arms, which were contracted—he spent maybe a half hour working on one elbow, just massaging it with his hands. He got her to extend her arm, a hugely important feat on her part, because it meant that with therapy—the kind of therapy we'd been begging Michael to allow—Terri wouldn't have to be shriveled up. Then he worked on the other arm, which didn't extend completely, but most of the way.

"Then he told Terri to open her eyes really wide. This is one of the most powerful videotapes we have of Terri. People that have brain injuries like Terri, it takes them a little longer. They don't respond immediately; it takes them a while to process the command. So you have to literally give them time to understand what they're being asked to do, and then to respond.

"So he's telling her, 'Terri, open your eyes really wide.' And he's repeating the command and repeating the command. Then you see him watching her and saying, 'Come on, Terri.' And then you see Terri open her eyes really wide, almost leaning out of the chair. 'Oh, that's great!' he says. I mean she opened them so wide, like saucers. And it was like, wow!

"Everybody was like '*Oh, my God. Look!* She just responded to him.' It was such an effort for her, and yet she followed the command."

Bob adds, "Then he had his hand on her leg and was pushing against it and telling her, 'Terri, okay. Lift your leg.' And while he was doing that, he was talking into the videotape, 'I can feel her pushing against my hand.' And she was! Which meant she can understand the command, and she was obeying his command to push against his hand.

"Then Dr. Maxfield examined her and put on some music. The videotape shows her reacting to the music by moving her body. It wasn't as dramatic as her reaction to Dr. Hammesfahr's commands, but it was striking all the same."

Bobby summed up.

"Five doctors examined her. Only three of the doctors videotaped—our two doctors and Dr. Cranford. And in every one of the videotapes, *Terri reacted!* The two doctors who didn't videotape her were Greer and Bambakidis. We had to go by their word. So when they testified in court, what do you think they said? 'Terri did nothing. No reaction whatsoever.' We couldn't disprove their claim because they didn't take videotapes of her. But I felt betrayed."

After the doctors' examinations, my fears lessened. After all, we now had visual proof that Terri wasn't PVS. Even Michael would have to admit it. Even Felos!

Instead, Felos immediately tried to get Judge Greer to keep the videos away from the media. Which he did.

The media aren't so easily put off. The local TV stations had their legal representatives in the courtroom, and one of them insisted that Greer had no legal right to deny his station access to the videotapes. Bob, who was there, remembers Greer's face going red with anger, the two men shouting at each other. The media knew the law, and Greer couldn't duck them.

He came back with a compromise. He wouldn't release the videotapes to the TV stations, but if they wanted, they could televise off the courtroom monitors on which the tapes would be shown.

The first witness in the October 11, 2002, trial was Dr. Victor Gambone, Terri's treating physician. Every time he was asked why he chose a particular course of treatment—or nontreatment—he answered that he was acting on Michael's wishes. Pat went to Greer after Gambone testified arguing that Michael should appear at the trial. For it was only Michael who could have answered Pat's questions: Why wouldn't he allow therapy? Why did he restrict our time with Terri? Why he did he deny her antibiotics when she had her UTI? But Felos was determined that he not take the stand. Greer denied Pat's request, and Michael stayed out of sight.

We were all convinced that Michael was avoiding questioning, but oh, how I wanted him to testify! His lawyer had referred to Terri as a vegetable, a houseplant—descriptions that stuck my heart like thorns. What would *Michael* say after he was shown the videotapes? How could he dismiss the evidence of his eyes?

Dr. Hammesfahr described his examination of Terri; how she responded to his physical therapy and to his commands. He stated she did not collapse from a heart attack.

Pat asked him what he thought she did collapse from.

Possibly from strangulation, he testified:

A: (Dr. Hammesfahr): Anoxic and hypoxic encephalopathies are characterized by multiple small strokes. So depending upon where that stroke is, is where your deficiency is. In your average stroke, the entire side of the body is affected. But in a hypoxic or anoxic episode, or cerebral palsy, you will see lots of different areas affected. And there may be another injury, a neck injury, which compounds her examination.

Q: (Pat Anderson): Compounds what, her condition?

A: Her condition, yes. There is a neck injury. There may be spinal cord injury, also.

Q: How were you able to determine a neck injury?

A: By physical examination. On physical examination, she has several characteristics that are not typical of a stroke. First, she has very severe neck spasms. That's typical of the body's response, splinting the area to prevent injury to that area.

Q: Splinting the area?

A: Yeah. If you injure your arm, you will move it. Your muscles will contract around it to keep that area from moving. Her muscles around the neck are heavily contracted to help prevent movement around that area. Later on in the videotape, we actually show that it's almost impossible for her to bend her neck. You can pick her entire body up off the bed just by putting pressure on the back of the neck area, which is not typical in brain injury patients but in neck injury patients. In addition, her sensory examination is nothing like a typical stroke patient or typical anoxic encephalopathy.

Q: Are you experienced in treatment of patients with spinal cord injury?

A: Yes, I am.

Q: You said you had never felt a neck like that except for one other patient, right?

A: Correct.

Q: What was the cause of injury in the other patient?

A: The person had an anoxic encephalous due to attempted strangulation.

A neck injury! Attempted strangulation! We hadn't known about it. Did this mean Michael had choked her?

Dr. Hammesfahr was on a "quack list," Felos said; his nomination for the Nobel Prize had been withdrawn. But Hammesfahr's was the most cogent explanation for Terri's collapse, and we believed him.

Felos argued that the tapes showed Terri as *un*-responsive, that there were hours of video that showed her unmoved by anyone or anything around her. True enough. But as Pat stressed time and again, Florida law says that for a patient to be declared PVS, she must be shown to have *absolutely no interaction* with her environment. Ever. The tapes that showed Terri responding proved that there *was* interaction, at least some of the time. And that was all that was necessary.

Dr. Cranford, whose tapes we used to show Terri was not PVS, and who was so encouraging to Terri when he examined her at the hospice, had testified frequently in major right-to-die cases as a proponent for euthanasia. All we had seen in the videotapes, he told the court, were reflex actions.

Cranford's testimony stunned me—it was as though he had said the sky wasn't blue. Am I insane? I wondered. Is he seeing the same tape I am? Does he remember what went on in the hospice? From the tape, Pat had blown up a picture of Terri looking adoringly at me, which she kept on display in the courtroom—it was the picture that became famous nationwide. Cranford said there was no way Terri could recognize me. Her reaction was "an involuntary subcordal response." He branded the picture as "cheap sensationalism—I've seen it done over and over again." Pat was so disgusted she stopped questioning him.

I felt that he had dishonored my bond with my daughter. How *dare* he claim Terri's look of love, which she never gave to anyone else, was reflex? I wanted him to apologize to Terri and to me. He had taken something pure and covered it with mud.

Exactly a month after the end of the trial, Greer ruled against Terri. Once again we learned that the feeding tube was to be removed. The date set this time was January 3, 2003.

Pat Anderson had expected this ruling. Over the course of the trial, she had come to believe that out of anger, humiliation, stubbornness—whatever—no amount of evidence would sway Judge Greer.[3] He had conducted the hearing only because he had

---

3   Greer also relied on the testimony of the "impartial" doctor, Bambakidis, who sided with Michael. Soon after, we found out that Felos and Bambakidis's brother belonged to the Order of American Hellenic Educational Progressive Association—but we couldn't find conclusive evidence that Felos influenced Greer to pick him. As far as we know, this was the only trial Bambakidis testified in as an "expert witness."

been ordered to by the appellate court, but he was going through the motions, she felt. This isn't a case to determine whether she was PVS or not, Greer said in his ruling (though it patently was). This is a case to determine whether she can be helped by rehabilitation. He admitted that Terri showed "signs of cognizance," but that they were not enough to prove Terri wasn't PVS.

It was clearly not a trial to determine what had caused Terri's collapse. In her preparation, Pat had gone through thousands of pages of medical information and so must have initially missed the MediPlex bone scan, conducted in 1991, which showed bruises on Terri's bones that indicated possible abuse, perhaps over a span of years. After the trial, however, haunted by Hammesfahr's testimony that Terri might have been strangled, she asked two volunteer nurses to go through the records again. One of them, Eleanor Drechsel, discovered the bone scan in one of the boxes containing Terri's medical records handed over to Pat by Michael's attorneys.[4]

Pat called us. "You're not going to believe this. There was evidence that Terri might have had broken bones all over her body."

The news made me frantic. Had my daughter been the victim of ongoing marital abuse? Had she covered up marks as so many abused women do, and kept quiet about it? It was too much; I could not believe it was true.[5]

---

[4] Multiple boxes of documents were handed over to our initial attorneys. When Pat took over the case, she found them disorganized and out of chronological order. In his book *Litigation as Spiritual Practice*, Felos describes the maneuver as "the discovery game … Bury the smoking gun in a mountain of evidence … You strategically place your client's incriminating internal memo among thousands of useless but similar looking data … do everything possible to give up as little they can."

[5] I do remember Terri having bruises on her arms and legs. She said they came from roughhousing with Michael.

Bob could. "In 1990, you and Michael were joined at the hip," he told me. "You knew everything, supposedly. When I heard about the bone scan and the fact they'd found all those bruises, I figured that Schiavo was hiding the scan and the fact they'd found all those bruises. Mediplex might have hidden it if they were responsible for the bruises. If Michael had caused the bruises, however, then their silence helped him."

Before Judge Greer issued his ruling on the trial to determine if Terri was PVS, Pat filed a motion requesting time to investigate the recent evidence suggesting that Terri's heart failure might have been caused by physical abuse.

Her plea was passionate: "Look, the very person who's trying to have her feeding tube removed—the very person who's trying to kill her—might have put her in this condition in the first place." She asked for a discovery period to find out what the bone scan was all about.

Greer denied the motion. The evidence was interesting, he granted, but irrelevant to the question of whether Terri's feeding tube should be removed.

While Greer didn't follow up on the possibility that Michael had abused Terri, the media did. "Do you think Michael did this to your sister?" they asked Bobby.

"It is still undetermined what caused Terri's collapse," he said. "However, the growing amount of evidence suggests that something violent might have happened to Terri the night she collapsed. Surely the question calls for a thorough investigation."

The investigation has never been made.

Pat would use the doctors' hearing, particularly the videos of Terri, to build up a solid record so that we'd have the strongest possible case when we appealed. She was actually cheerful as the trial progressed. But I, more than any of my family, became gloomier, more depressed. *How much hope do I have in me?* I wondered. *How many trials are there going to be?*

As it turned out, what changed our lives had less to do with the appeal than with the perception of the public. Forces I was only dimly aware of were beginning to emerge.

Chapter 14

Frustrations

*W*hen the doctors' trial started, we were struck by the fact that there were so many people, friends and strangers, on our side of the courtroom and so few on Michael's. The reporters, who had taken up the story and whom Bobby recognized, sat on Michael's side because there was no more room on ours. We would at least have emotional support, I thought, if not Greer's.

One of the most vocal supporters was Glenn Beck, who had left Florida for Philadelphia when his talk show went national. He set up shop at one of the restaurants across the street from the courthouse, and he sometimes came into the courtroom, the better to give his listeners an accurate picture of what was happening.

When the videos came on, showing Terri responsive, I looked at Glenn. The audience was gasping, murmuring, turning to each other, weeping, cheering—the commotion was out of a Hollywood movie—but Glenn simply sat there, his eyes on a monitor, tears streaming down his face. He was crying—it seemed like he couldn't stop. I looked at the monitor myself, and when I turned back to see him, he was gone, I suppose to tell his listeners what he had just seen. But I'll never forget his tears and what they meant to me.

We began to receive messages of support from across the country. We put the picture of Terri looking at me on our website, and the videos of Terri responding and interacting drew an emotional and passionate response.

I was deeply touched by the public's voice. It didn't matter to many of those we heard from what Terri's actual condition was, or to what extent she would recover. They simply understood a mother's love and devotion. When I read the court transcripts today, I'm struck by how emotionless they are, how bloodless. I realize they are meant to be factual documents. The messages from the public showed the other side, the emotional side. The letter writers empathized with the pain in my soul; to them, the law was secondary.

Nevertheless, it was in court that the battle for Terri's life would go on.

After a dizzying four months of motions and appeals, Greer's ruling on the October doctors' trial was scheduled for oral review by the appellate court. These were cruel days. As each decision came down, I felt tossed and turned by a whirlwind that would not stop blowing, one day encouraged, the next depressed, my mood dependent on the actions of lawyers and judges whose language I barely understood.

Pat went into the appellate court on April 4 full of optimism. She had provided the appellate judges with CDs made from the doctors' videotapes, which were clearer and had more definition than anything seen in Judge Greer's courtroom, and she now expected a favorable verdict. The judges this time were Altenbernd (once again) and new arrivals Carolyn K. Fulmer and Thomas E. Stringer. Altenbernd looked like the king of the court when he walked in. His presence was ominous. If anything, he seemed angry.

Our side, as usual, was packed with our supporters, Michael's with few. Michael himself was there (he seldom came to the hearings, and indeed showed up less and less as time went on) and more of the press. The national news services had picked up Terri's story, and there were continuous pieces on local television, but the national networks were not yet interested.

The judges sat down. "I viewed the videotapes of Theresa Schiavo and I didn't see anything there," Judge Altenbernd announced.

I look at Pat. She had melted like a snowman in the blazing sun. The courtroom went quiet. Pat didn't know what to say, what to do.

It's peculiar, but I don't remember my own emotions when Altenbernd said those devastating words. I had melted along with Pat, incapable of feeling, incapable of thought.

The court criticized us for failing to provide adequate evidence for our argument, in particular why we hadn't included testimony from Dr. Jacob Green, one of the neurologists who had sided with us earlier.

This made Pat all the angrier because the only reason we didn't was that Green had recently had hip replacement surgery and couldn't make the trip.

On June 6, 2003, the appellate court affirmed Judge Greer's ruling.

Two weeks later, Pat filed for a full appellate court hearing. Denied. But the court later granted Terri the thirty-day stay so Pat could appeal to the Florida Supreme Court. To do so, she would need new evidence, new facts. The court would not overturn the appellate court's decision unless we had them.

With time running out, we were forced into desperate measures.

A year earlier, in 2002, Bob had learned of a Texas-based therapist, Dr. Joseph Champion, who was doing state-of-the-art speech therapy with patients like Terri.

"One day I smuggled in an audiotape recorder and put Terri on the cell phone with him," Bob remembers. "Terri talked to him. She wasn't saying words, just making sounds—you couldn't understand what she was saying.

"All of a sudden I see Terri rise up and almost fall out of her chair. When I grabbed her and sat her back down, I took the phone and put the earplug in my ear.

"'What in the world did you say to Terri?' I asked Dr. Champion.

"'I told her, if she doesn't get out of her chair, they're going to kill her.'

"The reason I was making the tapes," Bob went on, "was so I could get them to Pat's paralegal, Tom Broderson. He'd make copies and send them out to speech therapists across the country." Champion's testimony wouldn't have held as much weight, Pat told us, because the therapy he was practicing was experimental, less in the mainstream.

One of the people Broderson sent the tapes to was Sara Green Mele, a speech/language therapist at the renowned Rehabilitation

Institute of Chicago, who wrote an affidavit saying that within a reasonable degree of clinical probability, Terri would be able to comprehend spoken language and follow one-step commands—if she were given appropriate therapy and training. Pat and Broderson also included information on Terri's ability to swallow, and in her affidavit, Mele added that she thought Terri could do so—a vital piece of the growing evidence that contradicted the diagnosis of PVS.

This was the kind of ammunition Pat was looking for. So Bob brought in a videotape recorder to show Terri moving and responsive. "I was a nervous wreck," he says. "The hospice people were keeping a closer watch on us. And I'm sitting there and I'm glancing at the door for fear I'm going to be caught, because if they catch me, I'm out of the hospice forever. It was a tremendous risk, making that tape, but it showed that Terri wasn't PVS, so it was worth it. I sent it to Pat the next day."

To combat Michael, we kept going back to his testimony in the medical malpractice trial. The money he promised to spend on Terri's rehabilitation was now being used to try to kill her, an irony I found particularly painful.

Bobby had an acquaintance who worked in a district attorney's office.

"My friend looked specifically at Michael's testimony during the medical malpractice trial," Bobby says, "and then he looked at what Michael had said and done afterwards, and he felt that Michael had definitely defrauded the court when he refused to use the money he won for Terri's rehabilitation. He also looked at evidence that Michael might have caused Terri's collapse. We had Cindy Shook's deposition, for example, even before the MediPlex bone scan. He wasn't sure we had a strong case there, for we only had circumstantial evidence, but he was sure Michael had committed fraud. But there was a statute of limitations on fraud and it was now ten years after Michael's testimony. He urged us to put everything we had together *fast* and get it to Pinellas County State Attorney Bernie McCabe."

Bob compiled a file with all the relevant facts, including his belief that the bone scan showed that Terri had been abused, and sent it on. A week later, he got a call from a Robert Lewis in McCabe's office: "There are no crimes to investigate further," Lewis told Bob. Even though Michael had indeed vowed under oath to take care of Terri, it was not illegal for him to change his mind.

Pat determined to take the case to McCabe's superior, Florida Attorney General, Charlie Crist, and had her assistant, Tom Broderson, call Lewis for a copy of his report.

Lewis said there was no written record of his investigation and there wasn't going to be one because all of those allegations had already been adjudicated. When Tom said, "No, that's not so," Lewis said he was misrepresenting the facts and hung up on him.

Pat told us that we probably should have gone to the police to file a formal complaint before we contacted McCabe. It didn't seem too late to try, though. Bob called the St. Petersburg Police Department. "I know the case," the detective who answered told him. "There's nothing to investigate."

"The police *have* to take your report," Pat said. So Bob, Bobby, and Suzanne marched down to police headquarters.

They were met by an officer named Strong. Bobby was the spokesperson:

"She basically wondered why I was filing a report thirteen years after the fact. I explained why. She created a file for it and said it would be processed."

We found out that our report went directly to the same detective Bob had spoken to on the phone, the man who had told him there was nothing to investigate. The matter ended right there.

We had one final shot: the Florida Department of Law Enforcement. They read the report Bob had given to McCabe and the St. Petersburg Police. There are definite grounds to conduct an investigation, a department representative said, and promised to do what he could.

He later contacted us, apologetic. His superior had told him not to pursue the case—his hands were tied. We discovered later that if he *had* investigated it, he would have lost his job.

I suspect this next part will sound bitter. And this is a book meant to honor Terri, not to get back at the officials who made uncovering the truth impossible. Still, the connections between the people who hindered any criminal investigation are too striking to go without mention. As Bob put it:

"It's a well-known fact that Judge Greer was a county commissioner before he became a judge. He had political connections in Pinellas County, one being Bernie McCabe, the other, State Attorney General Charlie Crist.

"We feel that everything was getting stonewalled, swept under the rug. We had the most unfortunate luck because the people who were in positions to help Terri were all friends and they were all protecting each other. And, in essence, protecting Michael Schiavo, who we still feel to this day could have been responsible for Terri's collapse."

Suppositions, yes. What's certain is the connection between George Felos and the Woodside Hospice. And the hospice was making Terri's life, and ours, more and more difficult.

Chapter 15

Hospice and Hospital

e visited Terri as much as we could during the spring and summer of 2003, sometimes as a family, often alone. Each time I went, I rejoiced and grieved: rejoiced because she was happy to see me, and I knew I was bringing her comfort; grieved because of the evident lack of attention the hospice paid her. She was bathed and her sheets were changed, and one or two of the nurses were kind to her, but she was being "warehoused," as it's called, and my resentment grew every time I saw her.

One day I noticed that there were goosebumps all over her. The thermostat in her room had been turned down to sixty-five degrees and there were no covers over her. She was freezing.

And she was being fed too quickly. The velocity of her intake, which was continuous from 6:00 p.m. to 6:00 a.m., and the position in which she received her food were crucial to her digestion. Yet time after time I'd see Terri lying horizontally while she was being fed, and the monitor of her intake showed 60 when it should have read 45. I'd push the bed up so she was sitting straight, listen to the gurgling in her throat, an indication she was getting too much food at once, and go to the nurse to complain.

"She's supposed to lie at that angle," was the response. But I'd prop her up all the same. In fact, no one did anything when I complained. Each time I visited, it was the same: the thermostat was down, and Terri lay or sat uncovered, as if she weren't human, weren't alive. Finally we went to Pat Anderson, who notified the hospice attorney. The implicit threat of a lawsuit made them raise the heat and slow the feeding.

Bob and Bobby thought the mistreatment signified more than mere lack of concern. By now, we had been receiving information from all over the country about cases similar to Terri's. One such patient was Robert Wendland, whose lawyer had shepherded his case up to the California Supreme Court before Wendland died from pneumonia. As Bobby put it, "There are things they can do to expedite someone's death."

"Yeah," Bob agrees. "Textbook. Euthanasia 101."

Pat urged us to have someone in Terri's room at all times—difficult to do since Michael cut down the visitors' list and ordered no visitors unless a family member was there. One of us would have to monitor Terri—no "outsiders," even if their names were on the list, could drop in to see her.

Then, on one horrendous day, August 14, 2003, we couldn't see her, either. She'd been taken from the hospice. Where? We weren't told.

Here's Bob's account:

"I go into the hospice. Terri's not there. And I ask the nurse, 'Where's Terri?'

"'I can't tell you.'

"'What do you mean you can't tell me? My daughter's not here. Where is she?'

"'I'm not *permitted* to tell you.'

"I literally pleaded with her. '*My God. Is she dead?*'

"'Well, I can't tell you.'

"'If you had a child'—which I know she did—'wouldn't you want to know where she was?'

"'I'm not permitted to tell you anything.'

"'Where's the administrator?' I shouted.

"The administrator appeared. 'What's the problem?'

"'I want to know where Terri is.'

"The administrator stared at me. I think I was so angry she got scared. 'Where would you send somebody if they needed emergency treatment?' she answered—and fled.

"I called Pat and told her Terri was in a hospital, but I didn't know which one. I was shaking. I don't remember being so terrified, or so angry, in my life."

Bob and I agreed to meet at Morton Plant Hospital in Clearwater, our best guess of where she was. She had been sent there before once when her feeding tube slipped out. Suzanne picked me up, and Bobby said he would meet us there.

Pat had called Felos, who told her Terri was bleeding internally; she had pneumonia and a urinary tract infection. But that's all he would say.

We got to the hospital around 6:30 p.m., went to the admittance office, and asked if Terri Schiavo was a patient there. They wouldn't tell us. "Well then," Bob asked, "was a young woman just admitted to the hospital?"

"Yes," they said, but wouldn't give her name.

Suzanne stormed out of the room, demanding to go to the executive offices.

"I just started to scream. *'Somebody's going to tell me where Terri Schiavo is and what room she's in. I'm her sister.'* I was going in and out of the executive offices. They were all kind of whispering among themselves. 'Just wait here,' they said.

"I was furious. 'No, I'm not waiting another second. My family needs to know what room she's in. She's ill.' You know, just ranting and raving and yelling. I probably went into two or three more offices before I found a woman who said, 'Hold on.' She took my driver's license and made a photocopy of it, then closed the door so I wouldn't hear her conversation. When she came out, she told me what floor Terri was on, but not what room."

The floor nurses wouldn't tell us anything either.[1] Michael had banned information of any kind; not even the number of Terri's room could be given to us. Imagine the frustration! But finally we found her room and went in. "Terri was pale and very weak, totally unresponsive. *I've lost her,* I thought. *All the hearings, all our battles, all our prayers. Useless.*

The scene stays with Bobby like a scar. "Terri looked horrible. She was struggling. Her breathing was very labored. And I said to myself while I'm looking at her, *You know, for somebody who supposedly can't respond, who's been labeled PVS or brain-dead, she's not acting like that at all. She's clearly in extreme duress, and suffering terribly from her condition.*

---

[1]   In fact, after we were prohibited from getting any of Terri's medical information, it was sometimes revealed to us by one of her doctors, a few sympathetic nurses, and in one case a discharged patient. In addition, we would sometimes see antibiotic fluid hanging from her IV, and so knew she was receiving care.

"I felt so bad for her. I didn't think she'd make it through the night. And part of me was, in a way, hoping that if she was suffering this much, she *would* die. But she fought like hell."

Terri survived the night. Her breathing grew stronger. We took turns keeping her company and making sure that she was well taken care of. Bob called the doctor whose name was on the bottom of Terri's chart, and we were able to get some information— maybe the doctor was unaware of Michael's orders, maybe he was just a good guy. And the next day, we finally got the details from Terri's primary doctor. The diagnosis: UTI infection; pneumonia; collapsed lung; esophagus bleeding; kidney stone.

Pat immediately filed a petition in Judge Greer's court for an emergency hearing to gain us physical access to Terri and access to information concerning her condition. Greer agreed to hear the arguments on August 21.

Then, for no apparent reason, Michael banned Suzanne and Bobby from Terri's room. The nursing staff wouldn't even allow Suzanne to peek in from the hallway. And he banned Terri's spiritual advisor, Monsignor Thaddeus Malanowski, from ever seeing her again.

Monsignor Malanowski, six foot two with carefully groomed white hair—a statesman—was a weekly visitor to Terri's hospice room for the five years she had been a patient there. A retired military chaplain, he was the only priest in the diocese who made the effort to comfort Terri and us. He was, of course, on our visitors' list, but could not go into Terri's room when we weren't there.

Without our telling him, he heard that Terri was sick, and he went by himself to the hospital. The staff got hysterical and almost literally threw him out. They told him Michael had specifically banned him, claiming that he was getting medical information during his visits and was passing it on to us. Can you imagine? A monsignor! A general! Of course he wasn't passing us information. He was simply there as a compassionate man of God who loved Terri and wanted to minister to her. The police threatened to arrest him because he wanted to administer to Terri the sacrament of Holy Communion.

The day after Terri's doctor updated us on her condition, a second doctor told us he had received a warning from Hospital Risk Management for disclosing Terri's medical condition—and was told never to do so again. The next day (August 19), Pat filed charges with Greer that Michael was in contempt of the 1996 court order that forced him to release Terri's medical information to us.

On August 20, without any previous notice, Terri, who was still under treatment and very sick, was released from Morton Plant and returned to the Woodside Hospice. She shouldn't have been.

She still had pneumonia and the UTI. Her coughing wracked her body so violently I could feel it in my heart. But on August 21—and it seemed to us it couldn't have been a coincidence— Judge Greer canceled the emergency meeting he had agreed to, on grounds that Terri was no longer in the hospital.

Four days later, she was rushed back to Morton Plant with a white-cell count of 22,000 and raging pneumonia. Pat, who told us the news, was afraid Terri would die.

Terri's condition grew worse. Bob and I went with her to Morton Plant. Watching her was agony. She was clearly suffering; the coughing prevented her from getting any sleep; her moans were heartbreaking. Her needs were so acute we barely took note of the fact that the Florida Supreme Court announced they would not give Terri a "stay," nor would they hear her case.[2]

On August 29, though Terri was only slightly better, we were stunned when paramedics came to take her back to the hospice. We told them Terri was still seriously ill. Mr. Schiavo's orders, they said. We were powerless to prevent them.

This time, she was in hospice for less than a day. A night nurse noticed her oxygen level was low and sent her back to the Morton Plant emergency room. Bobby, who stayed overnight with her, told us she had trouble breathing. A few hours later, Michael again had her returned to the hospice. The cruelty of it—keeping her away from treatment—astonished us. She was like a rag doll shuttled back and forth between hospice and hospital. *She's a human being*, I cried out. Nobody seemed to notice.

Bob and I stayed with her for an entire week. All that time she was unresponsive. But this time, she was at least given antibiotics, and her condition gradually improved.

The antibiotics were restored not on Michael's orders but, in effect, on Florida Governor Jeb Bush's. With the date of the removal of the feeding tube approaching, we had stepped up our public relations efforts. Glenn Beck had been airing the facts about Terri in hospice, so the case was now an issue across the country,

---

[2] Additional stays had been granted, extending the date to October 15, 2003.

though it was still mostly Florida-based, a fact that could not have escaped the governor's attention.[3] Also, Pamela Hennessy, the invaluable organizer of Terri's website, had organized a petition on the website, asking the governor to intervene. Within days, more than 30,000 people signed it (that number later increased to over 150,000) and also sent emails and faxes to the governor's office pleading for Terri. Their phone calls shut down the circuits. And Pat, who had contacts with the governor's attorneys, applied what pressure she could.

The result was a letter from Governor Bush:

August 26, 2003

Dear Judge Greer:

I appreciate the challenging legal and ethical issues before you in the case of Terri Schiavo ... Our system of government has committed these decisions to the judicial branch, and we must respect that process ... I normally would not address a letter to a judge in a pending legal proceeding. However, my office has received over 27,000 emails reflecting understandable concern for the well being of Terri Schiavo ... I feel compelled to write in the hopes that you will give serious consideration to re-appointment of a guardian ad litem for Mrs. Schiavo before permitting the removal of her feeding tube or other actions calculated to end her life.

This case represents the disturbing result of a severe family disagreement in extremely trying circumstances. Emotions are high, accusations abound, and at the heart of this public and private maelstrom is a young woman incapable of speaking for herself.

---

[3] Glenn's loyalties to Terri and my family never stopped throughout the remaining years of Terri's battle to live. He remains a close friend and is someone my family will be indebted to forever.

I am disturbed by new rumors about the guardian's actions related to the current care of Mrs. Schiavo. It has come to my attention that Mrs. Schiavo has contracted a life threatening illness, and that she may have been denied appropriate treatment. If true, this indicates a decision by her caregivers to initiate an "exit protocol" that may include withholding treatment from Mrs. Schiavo until her death, which would render this Court's decision ultimately moot. While the issue of Mrs. Schiavo's care is still before the Court, I urge you to ensure that no act of omission or commission be allowed to adversely affect Mrs. Schiavo's health ...

It is a fine balance between Mrs. Schiavo's right to privacy and her right to life, both of which are co-equal in our Constitution. To err on one side is to prolong her existence, perhaps against her wishes, and continue the debate. To err on the other is an irrevocable act that offers no remediation ... I urge you to err on the side of conservative judgment to ensure that all facts can be uncovered and considered before her life is terminated.

I appreciate your compassion for Mrs. Schiavo's plight, and that of her family members locked in dispute in these tragic circumstances. ... I hope that you will consider appointing a guardian ad litem to ensure that the ultimate decision is based on facts presented clearly, unclouded and uncolored by personal interests of litigants.

Sincerely,
Jeb Bush

According to two reporters who were with Greer when the letter arrived, the judge read it, then crumpled it and threw it in the wastebasket. To us, it didn't matter what he did with it. Terri's medicine was once again given to her at the hospice.

And because of Jeb Bush's involvement, the nation took notice.

The legal battle continued on other fronts. More and more attorneys were taking interest in Terri's case. The national disability community joined our fight, filing amicus briefs on our behalf. Pat contacted Chris Ferrara, the lead attorney for National Catholic Attorneys, an expert in constitutional law used to arguing in federal court, who agreed to act for us on a pro bono basis. We thus had another important ally.

Chris is five-six or five-seven, young looking—in his late forties—and neatly dressed. Bob met him in Pat's office and heard his own words coming from Ferrara's mouth. "The case is an abomination," Chris declared. "The whole thing is absolutely outrageous. When they see what Greer's been doing, when they hear what the appellate court has said, not a federal court in the world will uphold them."

I wished I could be as optimistic as he was. We'd heard the same kind of assurances before, only to be knocked down by whatever court was involved, including federal court. Still, Chris was dynamic and self-assured, and we watched him expectantly.

On August 30, 2003, he filed a suit in the federal court in Tampa against Michael for conspiring to kill Terri and named the hospice and Felos as codefendants. He also asked for an injunction to protect Terri from Michael and Felos and for assurance that Terri would receive proper medical attention.

The hearing, held a few days later, was contentious. The judge, Richard Lazzara, kept throwing questions at Chris, reprimanding him for submitting a complaint motion that did not say how Terri's case violated federal statutes. (Indeed, he had worked too quickly in order to meet a deadline Pat had asked for.) Lazzara instructed Chris to refile. There was no discussion of the injunction that would have protected Terri from her husband. Chris was outwardly calm and courteous, but inwardly furious. The judge didn't seem to understand the gravity of the complaint, he felt, even though Governor Bush had filed an amicus brief with the court.

Pat was keeping up the pressure on Judge Greer. The Judge had told two friends of hers, both highly placed officials in Florida law enforcement, that he would rule against appointing a guardian ad litem. Why? Because Jeb Bush had suggested it.

Pat filed a motion asking Greer to recuse himself from Terri's case because he had illegally discussed his strategy with unauthorized outsiders, Florida Deputy Attorney John Carassas and Pinellas County Sheriff Everett Rice. Greer denied the motion and, later, the two officials denied they had told Pat anything. The good-old-boy network was in operation.

Meanwhile, Pat petitioned the court to postpone the death date of October 15 (two months later than the original date set by the appellate court)—indeed to forestall any death date at all—and to allow eight weeks of therapy for Terri. She attached an affidavit from clinical neuropsychologist Dr. Alexander T. Gimon, who had studied the video clips of Terri at the medical evidentiary hearing and wholeheartedly offered us his services. To this she added four nurses' affidavits that claimed Terri was not PVS. The nurses—Carolyn Johnson, Heidi Law, Carla Iyer, and Trudi Capone—didn't know each other, so the similarity of detail is independent and uncoached.

Because the statements are so powerful, and because what the nurses testified to was verified by others at Palm Gardens, it's worth quoting excerpts from two of the affidavits. Here's Carla Iyer's:

The atmosphere throughout the facility was dominated by Mr. Schiavo's intimidation. Everyone there, with the exception of some people who seemed to be close to Michael, was intimidated by him. Michael Schiavo always had an overbearing attitude, yelling numerous times such things as "This is my order and you're going to follow it." He is very large and uses menacing body language, such as standing too close to you, getting right in your face and practically shouting ...

To the best of my recollection, rehabilitation had been ordered for Terri, but I never saw any being done or had any reason to believe that there was ever any rehab of Terri done at Palm Gardens when I was there.[4] I became concerned because nothing was being done for Terri at all, no antibiotics, no tests, no range of motion therapy, no stimulation, no nothing ... One time I put a wash cloth in Terri's hand to keep her fingers from curling together, and Michael saw it and made me take it out, saying that was therapy.

Throughout my time at Palm Gardens, Michael Schiavo was focused on Terri's death. Michael would say "When is she going to die?" "Has she died yet?" and "When is the bitch going to die?" These statements were common knowledge at Palm Gardens ... Other statements which I recall him making include "Can't you do anything to accelerate her death—won't she ever die?" When she didn't die, Michael would be furious. Michael was also adamant that the family should not be given information. He made numerous statements such as "Make sure the parents aren't contacted." I recorded Michael's

---

[4] April 1995 to July 1996.

statements word for word in Terri's chart, but these entries were also deleted at the end of my shift ...

Any time Terri was sick, like with a UTI or fluid buildup in her lungs, colds, pneumonia, Michael would be visibly excited, thrilled even, hoping she would die. He would call me, as I was the nurse supervisor on the floor, and ask for every little detail about her temperature, blood pressure, etc., and would call back frequently asking is she was dead yet. He would blurt out, "I'm going to be rich!" and would talk about all the things he would buy when Terri died, like a new car, a new boat, and going to Europe, among other things ...

I have contacted the Schindler family because I just couldn't stand by and let Terri die without the truth being told.

And this, from Heidi Law:

I know that Terri did not receive routine physical therapy or any other kind of therapy. I was personally aware of orders for rehabilitation that were not being carried out. Even though they were ordered, Michael would stop them. Michael ordered that Terri receive no rehabilitation or range of motion therapy. I and Olga[5] would give Terri range of motion anyway, but we knew we were endangering our jobs by doing so ... We were always looking out for Michael, because we knew that, not only would Michael take his anger out at us, but he would take it out on Terri. We spoke of this many times ...

Every day, Terri was gotten up after lunch and sat in a chair all afternoon. When Terri was in bed, she very much preferred to lie on her right side and look out the window. We always said that she was watching for her mother. It was very obvious that her mother was her favorite person in the whole world ...

---

[5] Another certified nursing assistant at Palm Gardens.

When Olga was talking with Terri, Terri would follow Olga with her eyes. I have no doubt in my mind that Terri would understand what Olga was saying to her. I could tell a definite difference between the way Terri responded to Olga and the way she reacted to me, until she got used to my taking care of her. Initially, she "clammed up" with me, the way she would with anyone she did not know or was not familiar or comfortable with. It took about the fourth or fifth time taking care of her alone, without Olga, that Terri became relaxed and non-resistant with me ...

At least three times during my shift where I took care of Terri, I made sure to give Terri a wet washcloth filled with ice chips to keep her mouth moistened. I personally saw her swallow the ice water and never saw her gag. Olga and I frequently put orange juice or apple juice in her washcloth to give her something nice to taste, which made her happy. On three or four occasions I personally fed Terri small mouthfuls of Jell-O, which she was able to swallow and enjoyed immensely. I did not do it more often only because I was so afraid of being caught by Michael.

On one occasion Michael Schiavo arrived with his girlfriend, and they entered Terri's room together. I heard Michael tell his girlfriend that Terri was in a persistent vegetative state and was dying. After they left, Olga told me that Terri was extremely agitated and upset, and wouldn't react to anyone. When she was upset, which was usually the case after Michael was there, she would withdraw for hours. We were convinced that he was abusing her, and probably saying cruel and terrible things to her because she would be so upset when he left.

In the past, I have taken care of comatose patients, including those in a persistent vegetative state. While it is true that those patients will flinch or make sounds occasionally, they don't do it as a reaction to someone on a constant basis who is taking care of them, the way I saw Terri do.

Despite these affidavits, and others like them, Judge Greer denied the petition.

Pat knew, of course, that Judge Greer would deny any motion of hers. Her strategy was to build as strong a record as possible so that when Chris Ferrara went back to federal court, he could argue with new weapons, new facts.

On September 22, 2003, Chris filed an amended complaint with Lazzara in federal court, citing civil rights violations Terri had endured at Michael's hands over the past ten years.

To no avail. On October 10, at a hearing to rule on the request for an injunction to block the removal of Terri's feeding tube, the federal court refused to accept Terri's case, saying that all the federal violations had already been adjudicated in the lower courts.

The October 15 date for the removal of Terri's feeding tube would stand.

I spent the fall of 2003 in a downward spiral. Each new negative ruling was an emotional punch in my heart, the words of encouragement from Pat or Chris no more now than feeble whistles in the din of bad news. At one point, we were told that the federal court had agreed to take Terri into its care, meaning that Michael couldn't touch her. But our joy was short-lived. The federal court had only agreed to *hear* a petition to take on her case, not act on it. We went from heaven to hell in a heartbeat.

Greer had ignored all the evidence presented to him and was still pursuing Terri's death. I was very depressed, couldn't eat or sleep, lost fifteen pounds. I found it hard to talk, so I stayed quiet. My only solace was my family. We were never closer, perhaps because we knew we had to hold on to each other or perish.

As scheduled, on October 15, Terri's feeding tube was removed a second time. Michael denied her the sacrament Holy Communion.

Chapter 16
Groundswell

*T*here was no one day that Terri's case became a political cause, no one event that changed it from a family tragedy to the focus of a national debate. Goodness knows, we didn't ask to be in the eye of a hurricane. Our only wish was to keep Terri alive and to be able to take care of her.

To this end, when the momentum began to build, we took advantage of it. We didn't question the motives of the people who rallied around us and supported us. We knew we were being "used" by some politicians and the media for their own agendas. We were not so naïve that we believed everyone who claimed to be interested in Terri's well-being. We did not subscribe to every idea or every political cause championed by the powerful people who championed us. We did not differentiate the pure of heart from the self-promoters. As I said at the beginning, we were not political people—and we are not now.

The reason we ourselves went on radio and TV all the time was to correct misconceptions about Terri—that she was a "vegetable"; that she was on a respirator; that she couldn't go outside; that she couldn't sit or couldn't respond or couldn't function. Her dignity, as well as truth, mattered to us. *She was a living human being!* So we fought for Terri, loudly and publicly, believing there was no other course open to us.

The federal court, our court of last resort, had ruled against us. There were no more motions our lawyers could make, no more petitions they could file. Terri's feeding tube had been removed. Within days, she would die. So we were happy to be "used" if it meant postponing Terri's death. If the politicians and media pundits could help, we welcomed them, and we didn't stop to figure out who honestly cared and who was merely riding on the bandwagon. Together, their voices were loud and clear and moving, and we were grateful to them.

The voices grew in intensity. Every day we recorded the new events—court decisions, how Terri was feeling, what Felos and Michael were doing—on our website. The responses grew in number, but there was no way to know how powerful they'd be. Our aim was to get Governor Bush to act by invoking his executive powers, for he was the only person who could save Terri's life. But Jeb Bush was silent.

On October 9, 2003, six days before Terri's feeding tube was to be removed, Monsignor Malanowski conducted an all-night prayer meeting at St. Lawrence's Catholic Church in Tampa, asking the parishioners to pray that the courts would allow a stay in the removal of the tube so we could go on fighting. The prayers went unanswered. Or, perhaps, took other routes.

The removal was scheduled for October 15. On the eleventh, a friend told Bob that Randall Terry might be able to help.

"I had no idea who Randall Terry was," Bob says. "I called Kenny Blake, Mary's cousin, and asked him. 'He's an activist in the pro-life movement. Been arrested dozens of times,' I was told.

"That morning Pat Anderson had called me. 'It's over,' she'd said. 'There are no more rabbits in the hat.' So I called Randall, figuring I'd try anything. He lived in St. Augustine, outside of Jacksonville, and said he would come down the next day."

Suzanne points out, "We had a meeting Sunday night with him and his publicist, Gary McCullough. Randall organized us. He was compassionate, supportive, calm, and organized. We had a litany of things we needed to do, and everybody got tasks. He told us to rent an RV. 'You're going to be outside the hospice camping in it,' he said.

"Across the street from the hospice there's a long industrial-looking building running perpendicular to the street. The building contains individual storage garages. At the very front of the building is a little shop that sells all sorts of odds and ends. Adjacent to the building is a driveway and a space reserved for parking. The proprietors of the building owned the lot and wound up charging the people who parked there, including us. In a way, we didn't blame them. They were invaded by "The Schiavo Case." Stephanie Willets, who operated the small store, was herself a renter. She allowed us to use her store as a communications center and as a place we could go if we needed a respite. She volunteered the store, not only in '03, but again in '05, when the invasion reached a monumental scale.

"I ran around town trying to find an RV, and eventually we got a motor home and we parked it in the lot. We lived there for the next several weeks."

All of us shared the trailer during the day. Bobby would often stay through the night. And still more and more people showed up, sleeping outside the hospice, and after the hospice chased them away with sprinklers, they came back.

"Some things that happened were remarkable," Bob remembers. "I looked out one day and saw people running telephone wires into the lot. They put out tables with computers on them, tied to this little odds-and-ends store. And they'd go on the Internet. They had a printer and a fax machine right next to our trailer. One guy came down from Pennsylvania—a computer whiz. He was the person who set the whole thing up. It was a network. Started solely to pressure Jeb Bush.

"Monsignor Malanowski was there every day. When Terri's tube came out, he said it was the first time he'd cried since his mother died. We had preachers with us. This was fantastic. People from all denominations were at our side—all of a sudden, everybody was a member of the same parish. Everybody was united in a common cause."

"Randall Terry is a controversial guy," Suzanne says. "He has a huge following, despite a reputation for over-the-line tactics—we were told that he carried too much baggage and were urged to not associate ourselves with him. But to us he was a sweetheart, and thanks to his efforts, a lot of people showed up at the hospice. Our petition was obviously gaining momentum. It was being reported that the governor's office was getting inundated with phone calls, faxes, and emails. I mean, they were bombarded! The messages were literally shutting down their fax machines, the phones were off the hook. Now that Glenn Beck was national, a lot of other radio programs were talking about Terri's case, and everyone—Randall, the petition, the talk show hosts—kept pointing to the governor."

I vividly remember the day Terri's feeding tube was removed: October 15, 2003. It was also the day we met with Jeb Bush. Suzanne describes the circumstances, since it was she who—inadvertently—was the star:

"We had heard that Governor Bush was going to be in Plant City for a groundbreaking ceremony. Plant City is about an hour away from the hospice. Randall Terry handed me the phone and said, 'You're going to call his office, and you're getting a meeting with him.'

"I was mortified. 'I can't do that. I mean, he's the governor. I can't just call him.'

"Randall forced me to do it. I called the governor's office and got hold of Jeb Bush's secretary. 'I'm calling for the Schindler family,' I said. 'This is Suzanne Schindler. We are requesting a meeting with the governor right now. He's less than hour from the house.'

"'I'll call you back,' the secretary said, and in a few minutes she did. 'The governor will see you. You'd better get there ASAP. The governor won't be there long.'

"So we piled into my Toyota 4Runner—Mom, Dad, Bobby, me, and Randall Terry in his suit and cowboy boots, curled up in the back. My husband, Michael, drove. The media, seeing us leave the odds-and-ends store, followed in a dozen or so cars, wondering where we were going. The atmosphere was light.

"The car just flew. I don't think Michael ever drove faster in his life. The groundbreaking was for prefab homes for migrant workers. We stopped at a tree-laden area, not sure where to go. We walked toward a group of people, the reporters and photographers walking backwards in front of us, shouting questions and taking pictures. One of them slammed into a tree. We thought it was hilarious.

"We were ushered into the kitchen of a demonstration house, empty except for a bunch of folding chairs set in a semicircle on the white tile floor. The governor arrived along with two of his security men and Raquel 'Rocky' Rodriguez, his attorney, a short, no-nonsense woman I liked immediately. There were others in the room, but I never identified them. I was very, *very* nervous and I started to shiver, though it was a warm, beautiful day.

"We sat down and introduced ourselves. Dad shook the governor's hand and immediately began to cry. He composed himself quickly, explaining that the tears were a sign of his desperation. We made small talk, then outlined the situation. It was very stiff and awkward. The governor seemed genuinely sympathetic, but he didn't answer Dad's question: 'Is there anything you can do to save Terri?'

"I didn't say much at all in the beginning. In fact, I was getting restless. I thought, *Here we have the governor of the state of Florida. Surely he's in a powerful position.* So I blurted, 'Pardon me, Governor, but you have to know someone of your stature, someone who's even more powerful than you are, who can help.'

"A big smile came over his face. 'You don't mean someone in Washington that I might know?'

"I had forgotten he was the president's brother! It never occurred to me. I just thought, *Come on, this guy's got to know some*body. And then I realized what I said. I backtracked. 'No, no. That's not what I meant. I didn't mean—'

"By now, everybody was laughing, no one harder than Jeb Bush. The awkwardness was broken. In that moment, we were a team. Randall Terry stepped in. If I can find a way legally to save Terri, he asked, would the governor look at it? He said he would.

"The meeting was over. The governor hugged me and hugged Dad. Dad said he had the utmost respect for Jeb's father and his family, and tears welled up in the governor's eyes. 'So do I,' he said.

Dad said, 'The apple doesn't fall far from the tree,' and started to cry again.

"We tried to leave, but couldn't because the doorway was blocked by a sea of cameras and reporters, not only those who had followed us from St. Petersburg but others from Orlando, which was also an hour's drive away.

"So we had to give a brief press conference before they let us go back to the car and, an hour later, to the hospice and the continuing fight."

The crowds were suffocating. Well-meaning strangers came up to us in the trailer to offer advice on how we could prolong Terri's life after the feeding tube was removed. Women rushed up to me to ask how we were going to feed all the people outside.[1] It was as though they wanted me to be the hostess at a cookout—and my daughter was dying.

When I get upset, I can't swallow, so I wasn't eating. Food was the least of my concerns. "Listen," I told her. "That's not my problem. If those people want to be out there, they can feed themselves." Not very gracious, I'm afraid.

Lawyers would barge in, telling us to fire ours and hire them— that *they* knew how to overturn Greer's order. Doctors arrived telling us what to look for in Terri's condition after the tube was removed. "Check her heart rate." "Check her skin." "Check to see if her eyes are dilated." A woman told Bobby he should visit Terri with his mouth full of water and transfer it to Terri through a kiss. After he had visited Terri, she approached him again to see if he

---

[1] Actually, buffet tables were set up in front of the hospice. Food was supplied by church ministries, local restaurants, and ordinary people, all chipping in to help us.

had followed her suggestion. He told her he had. Not altogether truthful, I'm afraid.

Police were lining the streets around the hospice and guarding the hospice doors. Red mesh fences were set up along the streets for crowd control. There were some protesters making a nuisance of themselves, squabbling with the police and demonstrating with foul words and in exhibitionist ways that made us blush. (Father Malanowski kept making the sign of the cross, a subtle gesture we found endearing.) Some of them volunteered to form a human barricade so we could sneak Terri away. We told them to leave, and they did, but overall, it was difficult to distinguish our true friends from the attention-seekers. I felt that too many people were tearing at my flesh, wanting a piece of me for their trophy cases.

Suzanne recounted the family's position:

"For the most part, within reason, our attitude was, *You know what? All we care about is saving Terri. That's it.* Sure the media were using us, but so what? If the interviews were a chance to save Terri, if these people had a chance to save Terri, then so be it. We definitely had a line we wouldn't cross—everything else we used."

We did interviews all day long, not only with Christian radio stations but with secular stations across the country. We were handed microphones and cell phones virtually every minute and told to talk. "Interview this guy." "Interview that guy." Most of the time, we didn't know whom we were speaking to. Bob and Bobby were the major spokesmen. I tried to stay clear, but there were dozens of times I couldn't avoid them.

Bob was getting phone calls day and night, not only in the trailer but at our home. Nobody seemed to care whether he slept or not. He got calls from Massachusetts and Illinois militias who announced they were armed and ready to march on the hospice. A group of Australian mercenaries announced they wanted to fly in to take Terri out of the hospice. Of course we told them not to come.

On the fifteenth, the day Terri's feeding tube was removed, people held up a huge banner that said, "Gov. Bush where are you?" They had "Starvation Day 1" printed on it, and they'd cross it off to say "Starvation Day 2" and "Starvation Day 3," etc. It was on the news all the time.

Pressure on Governor Bush came from another ally as well. On the fourteenth, when Pat Anderson told us our legal options were exhausted, Bob contacted the Gibbs Law Firm after hearing from several supporters that they might be able to help. Shortly thereafter, Bob and I got a call from an attorney at Gibbs, who asked if we could come to his office at ten that evening.

We had mixed emotions about seeing a lawyer that late. We were bone-tired and would have preferred to stay in the trailer. Besides, we were not very familiar with the Gibbs firm and couldn't imagine what the attorney had in mind. Yet Bob thought about how reluctant he was to do the TV interview in 2001. If he hadn't, he wouldn't have found Cindy Shook and Terri would be dead. So at ten o'clock on the night before Terri's tube was to come out, we drove over to the Gibbs offices in Seminole, not far from the hospice.

"The room was surprisingly large with a full-width glass wall overlooking a garden of flowers and tropical plants," Bob remembers. "In the center was a conference table that comfortably sat eight attorneys. In fact, there must have been sixteen, eighteen lawyers, some standing around the perimeter of the room. The meeting was led by David Gibbs and his father. They asked us to sit down and tell them everything we could about Terri's case. For the next couple hours, we reviewed the case, answering questions along the way. By the time we finished, it was after midnight. Mary was out-and-out spent, and I was pretty darn tired myself. But the attorneys were bright-eyed and full of energy.

"Unbeknownst to me—and I only found this out recently—they stopped doing all their other legal work and for a week concentrated on Terri's case. Gibbs was doing this out of his own conviction and the goodness of his heart. They had contact with the legislators and wrote the initial legislative bill that was eventually presented to the Florida Legislature. And they were also trying to get the governor to act. They wrote him letters explaining how he could use his executive powers to get Terri's feeding tube reinserted by taking her into his own custody.

"And still Bush hesitated."

After Terri's feeding tube had been removed, Michael's other lawyer, Deborah Bushnell, told us we couldn't go into Terri's room unless we were escorted by one of his representatives, and the police were on hand to make sure we didn't disobey.

One day when I went in—this was after the tube had been taken out and Terri was starving to death—Jodi Centonze's mother was sitting there, knitting! Another time, Centonze's sister was there reading a magazine. They were so casual, cavalier, waiting for Terri to die. They ignored me. It was the coldest, most unfeeling behavior I'd ever seen.

Chapter 17

Another Reprieve

*E*ven after Terri's feeding tube had been removed, I knew in my heart that something good was going to happen. And I kept saying every day when I woke up, "Today's the day Terri's going to have her feeding tube reinserted." I just kept praying and praying and praying and telling God, "They can't let her die. She doesn't deserve to die. She just needs help because she's handicapped. They can't starve her to death." *This is insanity,* I wanted to scream.

What I saw was appalling. Even after they had removed Terri's tube, they were trying to hurry her death. When I would go to the hospice at night to visit her, before I went back to the trailer, she would be lying on her bed dressed in corduroy pants and a turtleneck sweater, blankets up to her neck. And it was hot—*hot!*—and her sweat would just be dripping off her.

Don't forget. She was given no water, no hydration, and whatever water was in her they were sweating out of her. I would pull down the blanket, and I'd be screaming, "Put her in a nightgown!" It happened three nights in a row, the same thing.

The police in the room? They were there not to protect her, but to make sure we didn't help her, even though she was sweating and miserable, and human decency should have been enough to ease her suffering. After a few days, Terri's lips became chapped and dry, and I tried to put some Vaseline on them. I don't remember which member of Jodi Centonze's family was there, but I remember a policeman. He came flying across the room and stopped me. Stopped me from putting salve on my daughter's cracked lips.

The effect on my family was devastating.

"I would go to bed at night," Bobby says, "either in the trailer or at home, and sleep for a few hours. I'd just pass out, exhausted. There would be times I'd break down, crying. And when I woke up in the morning, I didn't want any noise. No talking, no radio on—only silence. When I was getting ready to go to the hospice, I felt like I was getting dressed in slow motion. It was a weird, surreal feeling. You got up at five, six, after two or three hours' sleep, and your head felt like it was going to explode. Your body felt like it had been in a boxing match with Tyson, and you had so much on your mind you couldn't think straight. You weren't doing anything, but the emotional drain seemed to slow everything down, and the smallest thing—shaving, pouring a glass of water, even walking—was an effort. But you had to run the gauntlet, face the press, do the radio interviews, go through the guards at the hospice to get to Terri, and so you forced yourself to go on. Every day, go on."

"I tried to get back to some sense of normalcy when I got home," Suzanne says. "I had my ten-year-old with me. I helped her with her homework. I made sure she took her shower and brushed her teeth and went to bed on time. My husband, Michael, was there for me. The phone was ringing every minute, but I didn't answer. Of course I was thinking about Terri, about Mom and Dad, about all those people trying to help. I found it difficult to sleep. When I got up in the morning and showered and took Alex to school, everything still felt normal. Even driving to the hospice was fine. Everybody along the way was going about their business normally. But as soon as I made a left onto that road in front of the hospice and I saw the gazillion media trucks and the hundreds of people, I felt like I was hit by a ton of bricks. It was like driving into this other world, a freak world, a world I lived in until I got back home. And then I was fine.

"I started having physical problems. I was having chest pains and couldn't breathe. I actually drove myself to the hospital, and I was in the ER for several hours. They took all sorts of tests, but—no surprise—the cause was anxiety.

"When I was little, I was afraid of airplanes, afraid to fly, and we flew a lot. I'd look at dad and say, 'Dad, I'm scared.' He'd answer, 'Listen, I promise I'll tell you when you need to worry.' And I'd say, 'Are *you* scared?' And again he'd say, 'No. I'll let you know when I'm scared.'

"He never did say to me, 'Now's the time,' but looking at him during these days, I knew he was worried and he was scared. But during those times, he was stronger than he was afterwards. He was a rock."

"What was worst for me," Bobby says, "was seeing my parents having to watch their daughter. Of course your own heart is breaking for Terri. But every time my mom went to visit her, she would come out in tears. It ripped my heart out. I was enraged that I couldn't do anything to help and that they were doing this to her. And then seeing my dad so upset that Mom was upset, it was unbearable. *Unbearable!* And extremely, extremely stressful. The stress never let up."

It was terrible for Bob, too:

"Mary and I used to leave Terri's room. After those visits, she could barely walk. And the media was outside, with all those cameras lined up, waiting for us to come out the front door of the hospice. So I would help her sit down just outside the entrance—there was a little bench that was behind a column and we couldn't be seen. And we'd sit there and she'd cry.

"She'd sit there bawling and saying, 'I don't know if I can do this anymore. I can't handle this anymore,'—watching Terri die like that. And we'd stay there for maybe five minutes, until she got her strength back. Then we'd get up and have to fight our way back through the media, who were asking all kinds of questions like, 'Well, what did Terri look like?' and 'Is she dead yet?' I mean, we'd be bombarded with these unbelievable questions, until I'd get her through the media and back to the trailer, her comfort zone, where for the moment she was able to breathe."

With Terri, I'd break down. Otherwise, I tried to be calm. Suzanne was having these stress symptoms, Bobby was frantic—frantic and angry—and Bob was in torment. I felt that it was my job to take care of the rest of my family, to be strong for them. I wanted them to come to me if they needed help, and that I would be able to give it to them.

My brother, Michael "Mikey" Tammaro, came down from Corning, and he was the one who took care of *me*. Really, without family, not one of us could have gotten through that time.

And every night and every morning that Terri was starving and dying of thirst, I continued to pray. And I believe God heard me.

One of David Gibbs's attorneys, Matt Davis, drafted a bill in the hopes that the Florida State Legislature would pass it and that Jeb Bush would sign it, but there was no telling if the Legislature would even consider it.

Bobby, who'd been lobbying for Terri in Tallahassee, was closest to the situation. He, too, feels that God was listening.

"In the middle of all this chaos in and around the trailer, he remembers, "the week that Terri was getting starved to death, we heard that there was already a special session of the Legislature scheduled. It was divine intervention. If the legislators hadn't been in town, Terri would have died the next week.

"I had gone to Tallahassee a couple of days prior to Terri's feeding tube being removed. And I met with a friend of mine up there, Victoria Zepp—she knows the governor, and she's involved in a lot of political activity.

"I asked her, 'Vic, is there anything our family can do right now to save Terri?' And she says, 'Bobby, I'm going to be honest with you. It's over. There's nothing you can do.' I believed her. I despaired.

"But now we're hearing about this special session, and we knew what Gibbs and Davis were trying to do, and we heard news that the Florida Legislature's thinking of bringing up a bill about Terri. The emails, phone calls, and faxes were working. The voice of the people was being heard!

"On the night of October 20, 2003, the Senate began debating the bill passed by the House."

"We were in the parking lot, watching the debate on the government's website," Suzanne says. "Each of the senators was coming up to give their opinion. Some were arguing for the bill, some were arguing against us. 'Oh, no!' we'd say. 'Oh, it's horrible!' And the next senator would argue for us, and we'd shake our fists and give each other high fives and shout, 'Yes!' The debate went on past midnight. After a while, realization dawned. 'My God! It's really going to happen!'

"When the bill passed, I remember we all started to cry and we hugged each other. The crowd erupted in cheers. The media was all around us and the lights blazed and the crowd was cheering. Everybody erupted. It was like winning the Super Bowl, only much better.

"Several hours later, the Florida Department of Law Enforcement came. That was an incredible sight. After she had gone almost one week without food or water, they were taking Terri to Morton Plant to have the feeding tube reinserted. We saw the ambulance carrying Terri driving off with this police escort.

"I thought at that point we were done. Jeb Bush called Dad to congratulate him. The case was over. We had won. Our Terri would be allowed to live."

We thought the feeding tube would be put back in immediately, and we planned to go to Morton Plant to see Terri as soon as the procedure was over. Governor Bush signed the bill named "Terri's Law" and issued an executive order restoring Terri's nutrition and hydration. But we hadn't reckoned with Felos, who immediately sued Governor Bush arguing that the bill was unconstitutional.

Judge Douglas Baird, of the Sixth Circuit Judicial Court, denied the motion.

Despite Baird's ruling, Felos had beaten us to the hospital and told the doctors there that anyone who participated in reinserting Terri's feeding tube would be sued. One of Gibbs's associates, Rex Sparklin, was at the hospital, too, and he called Dr. Jay Carpenter, who used to be the chief of staff at Morton Plant, and told the doctors that if they *didn't* reinsert the tube, not only would they be sued, but they would be criminally charged for disobeying the law.

All this took several hours, with Terri still without food or water, but finally the tube was reinserted, and Terri received water that night, food the next morning.

Still, Michael and Felos were doing their best to torment us. Here's Bobby:

"They were playing hide-and-seek with her. The feeding tube was reinserted at Morton Plant Hospital, and I went to see Terri right afterwards. She wasn't there. They wouldn't tell me where she was. I called Mom and Dad and said, 'I don't know where Terri is. They won't tell me anything.'

"It was just harassment. I ran outside with Pat Anderson. There were press everywhere who had been waiting for Terri to come out. They didn't know where she was either. So Pat let Felos have it. 'These people are tormenting this family,' she said. And I added, 'I don't know where my sister is. I don't know her condition. They won't tell me anything.'

"Soon after that, they told us she was back at the hospice—so we went there to see her."

To me, these bedevilments were minor. Happiness filled my heart like sweet nectar. Terri was being fed, and while Michael had barred us from seeing her at Morton Plant and forbade any of the staff from giving us any information whatsoever, we knew that for the moment she was safe.

The tube was reinserted the day before Bob's birthday. It may have been the best present he ever received.

Chapter 18
Aftermath

There was little relief.

When Terri's feeding tube had been reinserted, Dr. Hammesfahr took Bob aside. "This is a dangerous time," he said. "You went through a severe crisis. But it's often *after* the crisis that trouble comes."

With my brother, Mikey, I took Bob to Hammesfahr's office for an examination. Hammesfahr's took his blood pressure and literally went white. "It's off-the-wall," he said. "I mean, completely off-the-wall."

In our forty-two years of marriage, I couldn't remember its ever being so high. Between them, Bob's regular doctor and Dr. Hammesfahr managed to get it down, but he was inactive for a while, and my brother acted as his surrogate, especially escorting me to the hospice, where perhaps two dozen people remained to keep up a vigil for Terri.

Dr. Hammesfahr also told us what to look for when we visited Terri. "You have to find out if the time off the feeding tube affected her organs," he said. "Liver and kidneys. Try to take her pulse to see if it's steady, and find out if she's urinating."

But getting information from the hospice people was impossible. Never in all our dealings with them were they this mean, this ornery. So we didn't know how she tolerating her feeding, if the hydration was making her sick, if she'd suffered any internal damage. As Bob said, it was almost as if they were mad because they weren't able to kill her.

But Suzanne was encouraged. "I thought Terri looked really good. She bounced back really quickly. Her face filled out. She was fine. And after that, we were more convinced than ever that she didn't want to die. Not that there was ever a doubt, but we said to ourselves, *You know what? This is Terri. Just fighting for everything she had.* She was amazing. And healthy. That's the thing that killed us when Michael kept on trying to end her life. She was *healthy!*"

We had the fear of God in us because we thought Michael would try, underhandedly, to kill her. I remembered the rushed feeding, the blankets and sweaters to make her sweat when she was getting no water, the order not to medicate, and vowed such tactics would never be used again. But that meant a family member had to be with Terri 24/7, obviously an impossibility, and my anxiety was overwhelming when Terri was alone.

"I was still trying to work," Suzanne says, "and the idea of somebody not being with Terri was haunting me. I kept thinking, *Oh, God, what if we go there and they've done something to her?* The pressure was unbelievable at this point."

"The stress got so bad that it even affected our family dynamic," Bobby says. "Dad and I had a terrible fight, just screaming at each other as though we were enemies. I don't remember what we were fighting about, just the fight itself. It shows how on edge we all were. The family might have crumbled if Mom hadn't kept us together."

Meanwhile, Felos was waging his own fight—to have the courts declare Terri's Law unconstitutional—and our attorneys were uncertain what the courts would do. The suspense added to the pressure.

"Pat Anderson was telling us, 'We don't know how long we can keep Terri alive,' because she believed the courts were against us," Bob says. "We didn't know if the stay was going to last a month, two months, a year, forever—we just didn't know because Felos and his army of attorneys were doing everything they could to ramrod the system to act faster. Not knowing if Terri was going to be alive for long, the way the hospice was treating her and treating us, the media still hammering us for interviews—psychological torture. Here Terri was, reprieved, and it was just about the worst time for me in the whole affair."

On December 3, 2003, some friends of ours threw a party to celebrate Terri's fortieth birthday. They set up tables in front of the hospice and invited the fifty or so supporters who had kept up the vigil for Terri to attend. It was a lovely gesture, another reminder that in this world, good people outnumber the bad.

We gave slices of cake to the hospice nurses, not differentiating between those who'd been obstinate with us and those who were kind. Then the family went to Terri's room, which I had decorated with cards and ribbons, and we hugged her and kissed her and sang "Happy Birthday." Terri enjoyed it—so did we.

Terri had hardly aged at all. There was some gray in her hair, but her skin was still beautiful and young-looking. There were no squint lines around her eyes, no furrows in her forehead. Suzanne was amazed that she had more wrinkles than Terri did. But I wondered how many more birthdays lay ahead of her if Michael and Felos prevailed.

Chapter 19

Dark Doings

Throughout the fall of 2003 to the summer of 2004, Governor Bush and his attorney, Ken Connor, worked on defending Terri's Law, while Pat Anderson attempted not only to have Michael removed as Terri's guardian but to take Terri's case away from the Sixth Circuit and Judge Greer's jurisdiction.

Professor Jay Wolfson at the University of South Florida was appointed as the new guardian ad litem mandated by Terri's Law. But his report, saying there was value in conducting swallow therapy and continued testing for Terri, went nowhere: Felos claimed that Terri's Law was unconstitutional and that Wolfson's appointment was therefore inappropriate. Judge Greer turned down Pat's motion to transfer the case to a different court. And on May 5, 2004, Judge Baird of the Sixth Circuit Judicial Court, without a trial, issued a summary judgment declaring that Terri's Law was indeed unconstitutional, but withheld action until the Second District Court of Appeals could hear Governor Bush's appeal.

I felt I was living in a parallel world, where a different language—legalese—spoke a set of incomprehensible rules. I felt no connection to this world, yet knew that Terri's fate would be decided by those rules, and not by anything that governed *my* world, where humanity has less to do with law than with the heart.

All I could do was care for and protect Terri as best I could, though it was becoming more and more difficult.

And Bob was worried because politicians on both sides were expressing opinions on the case, their often uneducated ideas duly reported in the media. If the case becomes a political issue between Republicans and Democrats, he said, the issue of Terri's rehabilitation will be lost.

Woodside Hospice was undergoing a renovation, so in December 2003, Terri had to be moved, along with other patients, to the fourth floor of an assisted-living facility, Park Place in Clearwater.

Terri's room was at the back of the building. You couldn't see it from the main road—this to discourage crowds from gathering at the front. A policeman guarded her door at all times, and we had to show our ID and leave our cell phones and purses with the policeman. I felt like I was entering a maximum security prison.[1] Nobody was allowed to visit unless they were with us, so what was she being protected from? Her family?

Terri's room was stark. It at least had a window that let in the sun, and I was able to decorate the room with pictures. But the staff was rude—and her care was appalling.

At Woodside hospice, at least Terri was presentable. Her hair was combed, she wore a dress, she was clean. While the senior staff, nurses and administrators, were generally hostile, several of the certified nursing assistants went out of their way to be kind, both

---

[1] We were told the hospice paid for the police protection. By the end, it added up to hundreds of thousands of dollars. We thought that the money used to "protect" Terri could have so easily been spent on her rehabilitation.

to us and to Terri; at Park Place, the CNAs were different. Terri looked like she had been discarded. Her hair never seemed to be washed. She wore terrible clothes supplied by the facility—that is, when they changed her out of her hospital gown at all. Sometimes they wouldn't put her in her chair, but they didn't know how to sit her up in bed, so she eventually developed bedsores and had to be taken back to Morton Plant. When she *was* in her chair, they moved it to a dark corner away from the window. Why? Because they didn't want people looking in, they explained. Into a fourth-floor window at the rear!

For the past fourteen years, calling every day to ask about Terri's condition was part of my routine. When Terri was a Sabal Palms and Palm Gardens, I'd often get a tidbit of information, at times enough to put my mind at ease. At Woodside Hospice, I'd call and get a polite, "Sorry, I can't tell you anything about your daughter." But when I called Park Place asking for information, they were not as civil. I was given the runaround. It was like shouting into a void. It made me sick. Once, Terri was taken to Morton Plant because her feeding tube had fallen out. We found out about it only because we saw that Terri was still wearing the hospital bracelet on her wrist when she was back at Park Place. I had called that day as always and was told she was fine. Fine? She was at the hospital. Another time she experienced a bout of vomiting. I asked what had caused it. The staff told me they couldn't give out information. Michael's orders. His control at Park Place was as absolute as it was at Woodside.

In February 2004, Suzanne quit as a stockbroker for TD Waterhouse. "I felt like I was chained to my desk," she told me. "There was just so much going on that I couldn't handle my life. I was having anxiety attacks. I couldn't breathe. Something had to go—my job."

Bob had stopped working in 2000. Bobby was still teaching at Tampa Catholic. I was tempted to leave the Hallmark store, but chose not to. For one thing, we needed the money; for another, I had flexible hours, letting me spend as much time as I wanted with Terri. Besides, the store was a refuge where I was able, briefly, to not worry about what was happening to Terri.

On one of his early visits, in January 2004, Bobby saw that one of Terri's teeth was broken in half, and she was in pain. Years earlier Pat Anderson had brought up that Terri's teeth were being neglected. Now her teeth were rotting, and Pat brought up the matter to Judge Greer to no avail. A short time later, Bobby ran into Terri's doctor. "What's going on with her teeth?" he asked. The doctor said he had contacted Michael about it. It wasn't until April—April!—that we got a letter from Deborah Bushnell telling us that Terri had five teeth extracted.

Each day, we reported on Terri's care on our website. People, outraged, started calling the Agency for Health Care Administration, and they sent investigators to Park Place. What happened? Nothing. They found Terri well groomed, her charts in good order.

It seemed the facility had put on a facade for the inspectors, she said. As soon as they left, Terri's care reverted to warehousing. We were told that some of the nurses and administrators couldn't understand that we didn't want Terri to die. And those who had come over from the hospice resented the crowds we had drawn and the bloody nose the press gave them. One local radio station had been reporting accurate information about Terri almost daily. One morning, they had Pat Anderson on, and our lawyer lambasted the hospice and its cruel treatment of Terri. Suddenly the station began broadcasting ads for the Hospice of the Florida Suncoast all day long. The reporting of Terri's story continued, but the live interviews ceased.

George Felos's tactics up to this time were underhanded, unscrupulous, and cruel. But what he did next—and Michael must have approved—was evil.

On the evening of March 29, a Monday, a local CBS reporter called Suzanne. "There was nothing particular going on with Terri," she says. "It was quiet.

"'Have you guys seen what's coming over the wire?' the reporter asked.

"'No.'

"'Mr. Felos sent out a press release accusing your mom and dad of harming Terri. Have you any comment?'

"I was stunned. 'Gotta go,' I mumbled, and hung up on him."

Suzanne told us the news. We had no idea what "harm" Felos meant. Bob found out almost immediately.

"The CBS guy called me up," Bob says. "Extremely friendly. Claimed not to be looking for an interview. 'I just want you to know what's going on. That you're being accused of trying to inject Terri with some type of foreign substance. The implication is you're trying to kill her.'"

The press release read as follows:

SCHIAVO PUNCTURE WOUNDS FOUND
AFTER PARENTS' VISIT

Dunedin, Florida, March 29, 2004. Immediately after a forty-five minute visit from her parents, Theresa Schiavo was found by medical personnel to have been the victim of numerous wounds, five of them apparently caused by a hypodermic needle. Mrs. Schiavo was found in a disheveled state, with her feeding tube wrapped around her back, and an allergy band pulled up very tight on her arm like a tourniquet. On one arm were four fresh puncture wounds, with another fresh puncture wound on her other arm. Also found were fresh scratch wounds over the puncture wounds, as if an attempt were made to conceal the puncture wounds.

What appeared to be a purple needle cap was found in Mrs. Schiavo's gown, confirming the belief that the puncture wounds were caused by a hypodermic needle. It is not known whether something was injected into Theresa Schiavo or fluids were withdrawn from her. Mrs. Schiavo has been taken to Morton Plant/Mease Hospital for toxicology testing and other blood work.

A forensics team [has] examined the crime scene, and the Clearwater police are investigating.

Mrs. Schiavo's husband and guardian [has] issued orders stopping all persons visiting his wife until the police investigation is completed.

For more information, contact Felos & Felos, P.A.— (727) 736-1402

Rage is an inadequate word for my feelings. Years earlier, two of the Palm Gardens nurses had said in their affidavits that they believed Michael had injected Terri with an overdose of insulin; perhaps this was his way of getting back at them. More likely, it was another fabricated incident created solely to bar our visits, thereby stopping the flow of information about Terri's medical abuse. Whatever, the insinuation that we had deliberately harmed her blindsided me. When a smear is so blatant, there is virtually no defense.

"Needle Marks on Schiavo's Arm Prompt Investigation," blared one headline. "5 Needle Marks Present Mystery. How, and Why, the Wounds Appeared on Schiavo's Arms," screamed another.

We called Pat. She said that she wished they had called her first, as a matter of courtesy. [2]

Instantly none of us, not even Bobby and Suzanne, who were not "under suspicion," were allowed to see Terri. I had no idea how long we'd be prevented from visiting. A lie walled us off. I felt as if I had run into that wall. The injustice was so immense I could barely breathe.

A criminal lawyer, George Tragos, agreed to defend us. The next day, there was a knock on the door. Two detectives from the Clearwater Police Department stood outside. I invited them in and called Tragos, who asked to speak to Bob.

"Tell them to get out of your house," he told Bob. "Don't you or Mary open your mouth to them."

Bob was very polite to the police. "My attorney says you should leave," he said. "And we're not allowed to answer any questions." "Fine," they said mildly, and left.

On Wednesday, we met with the detectives in Tragos's office. Bob and I were interviewed separately in Tragos's presence. Both of us could only tell the truth: We had never, would never, inject

---

[2] We immediately filed a grievance against Felos. It went nowhere.

Terri with anything. Yes, we had seen Terri on Monday, as we had on many Mondays. There was nothing special about the visit. Terri was the same as always. There was no elaboration, nothing to add.

Terri was released from the hospital that day. Every test came back clean. The doctor said that the marks on her arm were not fresh.[3] Nevertheless, the investigation continued, and we were kept from Terri and she from us for over two months.

This was the first time in my life that I hadn't seen one of my children for that length of time. Since we weren't allowed in, I feared she wouldn't be taken care of, and in fact she developed the bedsores that rehospitalized her. I pictured all sorts of calamities, imagined my girl lying helpless and ignored. I was sick to my stomach every day, barely able to function at work. She wasn't being taken care of, and there was absolutely nothing I could do about it. It was psychological and physical torment. It was hell. I prayed that she didn't think we'd abandoned her.

The police report, issued after some sixty days, completely exonerated us. One of Michael's lawyers, Deborah Bushnell, immediately questioned the report—we were still under suspicion, she said, and the ban on seeing Terri persisted, though we would be allowed in under supervision. (I'm not sure who the supervisor was supposed to be.) I would have been willing to accept the compromise, but Pat cautioned against it. She didn't want it to seem that we *needed* supervision.

We went to court. Even here Bushnell argued that we were still a danger to Terri. But—a miracle!—Judge Greer ruled for us. I

---

[3]   They might have been caused by the Hoyer lift which the nurses used to take her out of bed and put her back in each day.

guess he didn't want to contradict the unambiguous police report that said we were innocent.

From then on, whenever we visited Terri, we were hypervigilent. As we were getting ready to leave, we'd ask a nurse to check her carefully and made sure the police officer on duty heard her report. And the nurse would look her over: "Yes, she's fine."

Which, basically, she was. Although still unkempt, her bedsores had been cured and she was still responsive. I marveled again at her courage and her grit. There was no doubt about it: *My girl does not want to die.*

Chapter 20

The Pope on Our Side

*D*at continued arguing that Michael should be held in contempt for disobeying the 1996 court order that he disclose Terri's medical condition. Greer rejected the motion, claiming that our contention that Michael withheld information was "hearsay." And Judge Baird denied us the right to join with Governor Bush in defending the constitutionality of Terri's Law, a move that would have added our attorneys' firepower to his.

Still, on March 20, 2004, nine days before Felos's accusations against us, we received support from the most powerful ally in the Catholic world: Pope John Paul II.

From 2000 on, people of faith—and not just the Catholic faith—had been sending faxes and emails to Rome trying to get the Vatican involved in Terri's case. Similar messages were sent to the papal nuncio in Washington. Even we, who had been given the pope's secretary's fax number in confidence, wrote two letters on Terri's behalf.[1]

We knew that the pope rarely speaks out on individual cases, yet still we encouraged the effort, asking people with powerful lay

---

[1] This angered Bishop Lynch, who later went so far as to claim nonsensically that Bobby had attacked him during a radio interview.

friends in Italy to join our cause. When Catholics approached us to ask what they could do to help, we'd say, "Get people to write letters to Rome." If someone with religious faith sent an email from Colorado, or Hawaii, or Timbuktu, our answer was the same: "Write to Rome."

There was a family who knew the pope personally. Their daughter was about to receive her first Holy Communion and the pope himself had agreed to perform that sacrament. During their time at the Vatican, they told John Paul about Terri, but neither they nor we thought he would say anything about her.

Well, he didn't mention Terri by name, but in his March 20 address, he made it indisputably clear that we must never deny food and drink to patients in a vegetative state. "I should like particularly to underline how the administration of water and food, even when provided by artificial means, always represents a natural means of preserving life, not a medical act. Its use, furthermore, should be considered, in principle, ordinary and proportionate, and as such morally obligatory. The sick person in a vegetative state, awaiting recovery or a natural end, still has the right to basic health care (nutrition, hydration, cleanliness, warmth, etc.), and to the prevention of complications related to his confinement to bed."

No human being ever descends to the status of a "vegetable" or an animal, Pope John Paul said. "Even our brothers and sisters who find themselves in the clinical condition of a 'vegetative state' retain their human dignity in all its fullness. The loving gaze of God the Father continues to fall upon them, acknowledging them as his sons and daughters, especially in need of help."

Bobby found out about the statement during a Google search for Terri, something he says he does "a thousand times a day."

"It sounds like he was talking directly about Terri," he told us. "It's as clear as clear can be. There's absolutely no gray area."

The pope's statement seemed a blessing from God, and we felt humbled, thankful, awed, and wildly excited. "It's new evidence," Pat exclaimed when we contacted her. By the time of the statement, we had befriended several high-powered attorneys,[2] and they all agreed with Pat. Michael was denying Terri, a devout and pious Catholic, her constitutional right to practice her religion. "With all the things we've brought before the court, they can't deny us this one," Pat said. "It's one of our fundamental civil rights."

"They'll never turn it down," the lawyers said, "not with the pope on your side."

Pat immediately filed with Greer to have the feeding tube ruling overturned, and Felos fought back, once again via the media.

"It's a frivolous lawsuit," he fumed. "This family will never stop. How long has the case been going on? Four years! And Terri wasn't even a practicing Catholic."

This last was an outright lie, and Felos knew it. So did Michael, yet he, too, lied. A reporter for the *Tampa Tribune*, called Bobby. "Michael just did an interview with us and said the Schindler family never went to church a day in their life."

"That's ridiculous," Bobby said. "Preposterous. They got married in a Catholic church, for crying out loud!"

Michael knew that the entire family went to Mass every Sunday when the kids were growing up, and that our children all went to parochial grammar, elementary, and high schools. Bobby was an

---

[2] Many of them were associated with the American Center for Law and Justice, a group that had lent their valuable support to us in 2003.

altar boy. When Felos made the statement, Bobby was teaching at a Catholic school.

Nevertheless, the *Tribune* ran with the story. Six months later, Judge Greer turned down Pat's motion, and the Second District Court of Appeals upheld him. To them, Terri's religious beliefs were meaningless.

To me, however, the pope's statement was as meaningful as anything that happened in our journey. Throughout Terri's ordeal, when things were blackest, when it seemed sure that she was about to die, when I had lost faith in Michael's goodness and the fairness of the courts, my belief in God sustained me.

And here, miraculously, was His representative on earth telling my family that our battle was just, our cause sanctioned by God. The legal system failed us. A higher court lifted me up.

Chapter 21

Desperate Maneuvers

*O*nce we were allowed to see Terri again, nothing else mattered except saving her life. Thus the events in 2004—the legal battles, the frenzied phone calls with good news or bad, the generally useless effort on all our parts to introduce some normalcy to our days—are all jumbled in my head like some abstract collage. It was as though I'd been in a trance, standing in place as crises rushed past, indistinct and too often terrifying.

I now quit my job. I know I was increasingly worried about Bob, afraid he would succumb to the pressures of his involvement in the legal strategies that were an almost daily matter of discussion and to the increasing pressure by the media, anxious for any tidbit he could feed them. He was magnificent during these days, supplying the strength he had earlier credited me with having. But his relentless efforts to gather support, to think of ideas for the attorneys, to listen to the advice of well-wishers, to appear on television to rebut the charges Michael and Felos increasingly hurled at him, took their toll. Once, earlier, we had rushed him to the hospital emergency room after he fainted from the stress.[1] Now I was afraid he'd suffer another, perhaps catastrophic, relapse.

---

[1] It was after Felos's accusation that we had tried to hurt Terri.

Suzanne had a different kind of stress, having to maintain a cheerfulness she did not feel to protect her daughter, Alex, who used to visit Terri and read to her. I was amazed by Suzanne's energy, her devotedness to us and to her husband and child, her refusal to let me see her terror in case it added to mine.

And Bobby—well, my gallant son became a lobbyist, fighting for the survival of Terri's Law through the politicians in Tallahassee and for new protection for Terri from the politicians in Washington. He, too, had now quit his job to devote all this time to his sister. He seemed inspired to me, as though by trying to save Terri he had found his calling.

Through it all, I became more quiet than ever. I still had trouble swallowing or speaking. I prayed for Terri, and helped my family as best I could. I tried to stay out of the legal tangles and to focus on Terri—being with her, caring for her, making things as normal as possible.

We did make one last humanitarian appeal—a proposal to Michael relayed by David Gibbs to Deborah Bushnell and George Felos:

October 26, 2004

Dear Ms. Bushnell and Mr. Felos:

As new lead counsel to the cases surrounding Terri Schiavo, we are not aware of any recent attempt to resolve this matter among the family members without continued court intervention. In order to make certain that this avenue of potential resolution is not overlooked, we are providing you with the following proposal from the Schindler family ...

The Schindlers' sole desire in making this proposal is that they be permitted to take their daughter and sister home to care for her within their family. The Schindler family members would take on this responsibility at their own expense. In consideration of your client permitting them to take Terri home, they would be willing to provide him with any legal guarantees he would desire, including the following:

1) *The Schindlers would never seek any money from Michael. He could retain any monies or other assets that might remain to him, either from their married life together, from the malpractice awards for himself or for Terri, or any other assets he might have received in the past. They would not seek any financial help from him for any care, therapy, or rehabilitation for Terri.*

2) *The Schindlers fully understand and appreciate that Michael now has a new life with Jodi and their two children. If he would desire to divorce Terri, the family would sign any necessary legal documents to assure Michael that, upon Terri's natural death, he would receive any of Terri's estate that he would inherit were he to remain her husband. Whether or not Michael would choose to pursue a divorce from Terri, the Schindlers would guarantee that he could retain whatever visiting rights he might desire with Terri for the rest of his life.*

3) *The Schindlers would agree to forego any and all future legal claims or actions against Michael or against any of his agents in this matter for any reason.*

4) *The Schindlers would permit Michael's attorneys to draft any agreement regarding this matter that Michael would desire, including the above referenced terms and any other terms he*

and his attorneys would find appropriate, excluding payment of Michael's previous legal fees or costs.

Now that Michael is a father himself, the Schindlers are pleading with him to consider their love for their daughter and to permit them to take over Terri's care, with their blessings on Michael as he continues to live his own life with his new family.

Please provide a copy of this letter to Michael and respond to us within five days.

The letter was never answered.

And so the time went on. Pat Anderson, her associate Tom Broderson, David Gibbs, his associate Barbara Weller, and other members of the Gibbs Law Firm worked tirelessly on our behalf. David is married with four children, and we felt terrible he wasn't seeing his family. (We sent a basket of flowers to his wife because he was never home—small compensation.) Both he and Pat gave months solely to Terri's case, bonding with us, loving us, loving Terri. Goodness knows what it did to their legal practices during that time. They never complained but rather doubled their efforts. "What if we try …" "What if we approach …" "Is there a loophole that would let us …"

But finally all our moral and legal efforts failed. Terri's feeding tube was removed on March 18, 2005. And another maelstrom, similar to the one in 2003 but far greater in size and volume, formed around us.

We were more than national celebrities; we were—depending on one's political point of view—martyrs or crackpots. Huge crowds, far larger than the crowds in 2003—crowds larger than any I could imagine—gathered at the hospice and around the odds-and-ends store we once again used as headquarters. It seemed we had literally legions of friends, both famous and not. Each day, we were greeted with banners, signs, shouts, songs, and prayers.

Sean Hannity, the radio and television commentator, came down to St. Petersburg, not only because we were "good copy"— we were on his radio or television program virtually every night for more than a week—but because he honestly believed in our cause. Every day, he was nice enough to spend an hour or so with us before his programs and a similar time afterward, learning about the case and relaying the information to his listeners. When Bobby was lobbying in Washington, Sean called him practically every day for an interview. Glenn Beck, who had been our leading media supporter since 2001, also interviewed us frequently during this period. (So did many others, including Michael Reagan, Drew Mariani, and local radio personality John Sipos.) We felt that our story was finally getting out—and that listeners shared our outrage. By the end, Sean was starting to wonder what had happened to Terri the night she collapsed. "There's something more to this than the mainstream media has been reporting all these years," he said.

Jesse Jackson joined us for the last few days and prayed with our family. He even went to Tallahassee to talk to Governor Bush to see if there was any way to get the Florida Legislature to pass another bill. "You need three miracles for Terri to perform if she's to become a saint," Glenn Beck joked. "Well, we've seen the first one. Jesse Jackson and Sean Hannity are in the same room together."

About a week before the feeding tube was removed, Mel Gibson had put out a press release supporting our family. Now he called

Bob to offer support directly. So did Jim Caviezel, who starred in *The Passion of the Christ*. We heard from Rosalynn Carter. We got support from Chuck Norris, Patricia Heaton, Randy Travis, and particularly Pat Boone who has a disabled grandson. Ralph Nadar had expressed his anger at what was happening to Terri. We were told that efforts were being made in Switzerland, the Vatican, and Canada to offer Terri political asylum.

"I think everybody saw what was going on," Bobby said after Terri died. "An innocent, disabled woman was being unjustly starved to death. And when you have people of their stature, and the pope and the president, and the governor and senators and congressmen on Terri's side, and they are unsuccessful, you understand how powerful the death movement is in our nation."

After March 18, we didn't know how much time we had left to save Terri. Twice before, her feeding tube had been removed; both times, it had been reinserted and she seemed no worse. Still, our desperation grew hourly. Not only was it imminent that Terri's feeding tube was going to be removed, Judge Greer added a new order on March 8. He ordered that Terri could not be provided with food or water by natural means, eliminating any possibility that we could feed Terri by mouth. We knew that unless there was a dramatic change—unless someone of immense power could act on her behalf—Terri was doomed.

Terri's Law, which Jeb Bush had so willingly signed in 2003, had been declared unconstitutional. Since then, other than his attorneys' appeals, he had taken no real action. He was still a potential savior, but we were less and less hopeful that he would intervene. If a reprieve was possible, we felt, it would come from Washington.

Not only David Gibbs but a number of other powerful lawyers determined to work at the federal level.

Here's Bobby's account:

"Governor Bush's lawyer, Ken Connor, was involved. And Dr. Robert Destro from Catholic University. David Gibbs, of course. And Burke Balch, a lawyer from National Right to Life. They, and many others, were all working on a bill that could be passed by Congress which could save Terri's life.

"Obviously, it would have to pass both the House and the Senate, and they asked if Suzy and I wanted to go to Washington to lobby for it. You bet we did!

"It was arranged for Suzy and me to lobby with four women from the National Right to Life organization: Megan Dillon, Elizabeth Maier, Dorothy Timbs, and Lori Kehoe, whose tenaciousness made her an invaluable ally. We also had the help of the Dwyer family— Dr. Dwyer, his wife, Linda, and the voice of their disabled son, Christian, who was in a wheelchair. It was extremely difficult for Christian to travel, but he nevertheless felt so strongly about Terri's situation that he came all the way from Texas to help us convince Congress that Terri needed their help.

"Mr. Connor also met with Suzy and me and introduced us to Senator Mel Martinez and Congressman David Weldon, both Floridians, who were sponsoring a bill in the Senate and the House respectively that would guarantee Terri the right to habeas corpus.[2]

---

[2] A writ of habeas corpus is a judicial mandate to a prison official ordering that an inmate be brought to court so it can be determined whether or not that person is imprisoned lawfully. In family law, a parent who has been denied custody of his or her child by a trial court may file a habeas corpus petition.

If it passed, Terri's case would be reheard. At the very least, Terri's feeding tube would be restored, if only temporarily. It seemed to me nonsensical that convicted murderers would have the right of habeas corpus and Terri didn't.

"Suzanne stayed a day, I the rest of the week, trying to plead our case with congressmen and senators (and their aides) so they would vote for the bill. It was tough going. I said to Suzy, 'Where's the press? We're lobbying these people, trying to get a bill introduced, and we need publicity to get the bill passed.' I went home dejected, wounded by the disinterest of the people on Capitol Hill.

"And then, suddenly, the media found out about what we were trying to do, and the buzz started. I went back to Washington. This time, the reception was different. 'Bobby, be ready,' I was warned. 'You're going to get some harsh reactions. Don't take it personally.' But in fact, with a few exceptions, I was greeted with respect and often sympathy. What I and the lobbyists were trying to do was to point out that Terri's case wasn't just a pro-life issue, but a *disability* issue as well—that Terri's rights as a disabled person were at stake. Support in the form of faxes and emails from disability organizations across the country added to the pressure.

"The habeas corpus bill became problematic and was thrown out.[3] Congressman James Sensenbrenner of Wisconsin, chairman of the House Judiciary Committee, immediately proposed a simpler bill, specifically for Terri, which would afford her the due process in federal court she hadn't received in state courts.[4] The House passed the bill. The Senate passed a different version, which had to go back to the House. The bills had to be reconciled, with Iowa Senator Tom

---

[3] The technicalities then and now were too complex for us to understand. We were only interested in results.

[4] Judge Greer was the only finder of fact in Terri's case.

Harkin, a Democrat, instrumental in the negotiations. But by then, most of the House members had already left for Easter vacation.

"Frantic calls went out. Enough representatives returned to form a quorum, some actually from the airport, others from their Washington homes. It was after midnight on Palm Sunday morning that the bill passed, ready for George Bush's signature that would make it law. Indeed, the President was flying back from Texas to sign it.

"I don't feel I had much to do with its being passed. The legwork was really done by our attorneys, the bloggers, the emails, the phone calls, and all our supporters pleading with Congress to intervene. They deserve the credit. I was available to answer questions about Terri and to act as a spokesperson for my family. Looking back now, it was a privilege to be granted such an on-the-fly education. Then what I mostly felt was pressure building in my chest. Terri could die at any minute. There was no time for reflection.

"I was in House Majority Leader Tom Delay's private room at the Capitol, watching the bill being debated on television. I remember looking out the window. There was a full moon, or close to a full moon, in the cloudless sky. I thought, *I'm sitting here in Washington among the most powerful people in the world. The president is flying here in the middle of the night just to sign Terri's Law—to sign a bill that will save my sister.* It was more than surreal. I felt awed—and humble.

"Mr. DeLay hugged me when victory was sure. Representative Sensenbrenner came up to shake my hand, but I hugged him instead. He's well over six feet tall and virtually smothered me. Everybody in the room was laughing. I could see how happy they all were. And then we went outside the private room and were swarmed by the media.

"Burke Balch, the National Right to Life lawyer who had been so helpful, had told me earlier, 'Even if this bill passes, there's a chance that the federal courts could reject it.' So I was happy, but still frightened by what he said. I called my parents, keeping my reservations to myself. They were ecstatic.

"A few of us waited in the apartment of a friend for my parents to call to tell me Terri's nourishment had begun again. One hour went by, then another. I called Suzy. She hadn't heard anything. Then the doubt set in hard, and I started getting really nervous. At dawn, I went back to my hotel room. There was no news."

"Dad and I watched them arguing the bill," Suzanne adds. "We didn't have cable TV in the odds-and-ends shop, so we sat in the CNN truck, asking 'Did it pass? Did it pass?' Then Bobby called and told us it *had* passed, and everyone went crazy. David Gibbs called. He was on the way to federal court with the paperwork that had been faxed from Washington. It was just a formality, he said. The judge would sign it, and the feeding tube would be put back in.

"Dad and I went to a little room in the hospice to wait. Mom was home, and we didn't want to wake her until we were sure everything was all right—and there was only silence. Bobby kept calling: 'Hear anything?' The suspense was unbearable.

"Finally we called David, who was waiting at the courthouse for the judge to sign the papers. 'Don't worry,' he said, sounding upset. 'They had go wake Judge Whittemore up.[5] He'll come when he's had his breakfast.'

---

[5]   James D. Whittemore, U.S. District Court for the Middle District of Florida.

"That made dad furious. 'Terri's starving to death and the guy won't come to the courthouse until he's had *breakfast*?' Meanwhile, Bobby was flying home, going out of his mind because he'd heard nothing."

Eventually, Judge Whittemore decided that a hearing was necessary. Michigan Senator Carl Levin had inserted language into the Senate bill changing the phrase "*shall* issue a stay" to "*may* issue a stay," meaning that the insertion of the feeding tube was up to the discretion of the court. The House had refused to adopt the changed phrase (it was the reason the two chambers had to meet to reconcile the bill in the first place). Levin and Senate Majority Leader Bill Frist should argue the point for the *Congressional Record*, Levin said. Frist agreed, and it was Levin's argument that Judge Whittemore used to rule that a hearing was necessary.

"I wasn't at the hearing," Bobby says, "but the moment I landed in Florida, I called Suzanne. 'What's going on? *What's going on?*'

"'Oh, Bobby, the hearing was horrible,' Suzy sobbed. 'The judge was arrogant, ornery, and basically just painted a very bad picture. He didn't say when he was going to rule, and we're still waiting.'"

"*This is bad*, I thought. *This is awful*. I just couldn't believe it. Here we were with a bill to save Terri's life, and the court won't allow it."

"When Jeb Bush wrote that letter to Judge Greer," Bob said later, "Terri's case became politicized. The judicial branch fought with the executive branch and with the legislative branch, and Terri was nothing more than a pawn. The media made it a right-wing, left-wing fight, but that wasn't accurate. The bill to save her life was a *bipartisan* bill. Not one senator objected to the bill, and except for a few in the house, Congress voted to save Terri's life. The court let the few decide the issue."

Bobby describes a poignant episode, that, if anything, shows how *un*-political Terri's situation was for us.

"It was Easter Sunday," he says. "Terri had been starved for eight days. I was visiting with her. As I was about to leave, I gave her a big hug and said, 'I love you Terri, and I'll be back soon to see you.' Then I broke down and started to cry.

"When I got to the hallway, Suzy said, 'Look at your shoulder.'

"I looked. They had put Vaseline on Terri's lips to ease the dehydration, and the Vaseline had stained my shirt as I was hugging her and saying goodbye.

"I put the shirt in storage, never to wear it again. The impression of her lips remains on my shirt to this day."

Once more, a judge, in this case a federal judge, decided Terri should die. Earlier, Pat Anderson had described what she called The Rule of Terri: "If it will help Terri die, then we, the courts, definitely observe every nicety in the rule or statute or the case law. If it will impede her death, we will ignore it completely."

I think of these words often, and I think of the words of John Paul II. Which laws are right? The laws of man or the laws of God?

Our last faint hope lay in Tallahassee, where the Legislature was trying to come up with a bill, even as Congress was working on its own bill. Just prior to the removal of Terri's feeding tube, David Gibbs told us we had an appointment to see the state attorney general, Charlie Crist, followed by a meeting with Governor Bush himself.

"So we jump on a plane," Bob remembers, "and fly to Tallahassee. Well, Crist never shows, but rather sends in an assistant who apologizes for him. From there, we walk down the hall to the governor's office. David Gibbs is with us, but two of Jeb Bush's attorneys funnel him off to a side room, and we go to see Bush alone. The governor is gracious, polite, sympathetic. But he's not promising anything—indeed, he's not saying anything of substance. And I'm kind of looking at Mary and she's looking at me, and all we want to do is get out of there. Finally, he says, 'What I suggest you do is lobby with the state senators and representatives to get the bill passed'—and that was that."

I'm not a lobbyist by nature, and I was too exhausted, too emotionally drained, to muster up any energy for the job. We let a veteran handle it: my valiant Bobby.

"After I got back from Washington, there was still activity going on in Florida," he says. "We were having trouble in Tallahassee. A new bill to save Terri that seemed like a slam dunk ran into a roadblock. It passed the House, but State Senator Jim King, who was against anything being passed for Terri, had enrolled nine of his Republican colleagues to vote against it—enough to defeat it. If that weren't enough, even if it passed, it would have to go in front of Judge Greer. Still, getting it passed was a first step. So I flew to Tallahassee and started lobbying the nine Republicans. Again, someone from Right to Life arranged the meetings.

"The Capitol was mobbed. Several of the representatives angrily told me they were getting threats—pass the bill or you will die. 'Please believe me,' I said. 'Our family has nothing to do with this. We can't control it. But can you please understand why I'm here and how important this is?'

"Later that day, it went to the floor and was debated again. Terri had had no food or water for over a week. *If the bill doesn't pass,* I thought, *there's no recourse left.*

"It failed. Several of the senators apologized to me: 'We're sorry, but we can't vote for this.'

"I held an impromptu press conference expressing my sadness. Several of the reporters told me that Governor Bush was about to hold a press conference. The rumor was that he would take Terri into protective custody. Washington had failed. Tallahassee had failed. Was Jeb Bush going save Terri, after all?

"I felt a surge of optimism and hope: *At last, the governor's going to do something*!

"An hour later, I was taken to the room where Governor Bush was going to speak, but was quickly told to leave—only media people were allowed. So I went outside and waited.

"Jeb Bush didn't say he would take Terri into his custody," Bobby continues. "He did announce that William Cheshire, a neurologist from the Mayo Clinic, had evaluated Terri and found that she was not in PVS. Rather, he believed she was in a minimally conscious state—enough evidence for the governor to ask the Department of Children and Families to further investigate. I believed that Dr.

Cheshire's findings gave the governor sufficient authority to take Terri into protective custody—but he still didn't say that he would.

"I had started to leave, half hopeful, half discouraged, when someone stopped me. 'Bobby, come with me. The governor wants to meet with you.' Hope soared.

"Christa Calmas, one of the governor's attorneys, met me at the door to Bush's outer office. I had spoken to her on the phone in the past; now we made small talk. The governor's lead attorney, Rocky Rodriguez, came in and greeted me warmly. Several people I didn't know ran around, doing God knows what. The place was frantic.

"I was ushered into Governor Bush's office. Senator Mel Martinez was there. 'Hey, Bobby,' he said. 'How are you?'

"'Hey, Senator, how you doin'?' My pal Mel. Surreal.

"After Senator Martinez left the room I sat across from Governor Bush. 'Bobby,' the governor said, 'we're working on getting your sister fed right away, on getting her hydrated right away.'

"Joy exploded in me. 'Well, thank you, governor,' I said. 'That's great news.'

"Rocky Rodriguez came rushing in and spoke to Bush quietly. 'Rocky,' he said, 'whatever you need to do, get it done.'

"She left. People were running around. Christa Calmas was sitting next to me. I was making small talk with the governor. Then Rocky came in and said something else, which seemed to frustrate the governor. 'Rocky, you make the decision. *Get it done!*'

"Again she left. 'We have a few things we've got to take care of, but we're going to get your sister hydrated right way.' Christa told me.

"'That's wonderful news,' I said, and a few minutes later, we get up to go. I turned to Governor Bush and thanked him over and over again. I couldn't seem to stop thanking him. 'Please call me when Terri's getting hydrated,' I asked Christa. She said she would.

"I had flown to Tallahassee, but now rented a car to drive home. On the way, I called Suzy to tell her what had happened. 'Don't tell Mom and Dad.' I warned her. Christa hadn't called yet.

"About forty-five minutes later, my cell phone rang. It was Christa. 'We've run into some problems,' she said. 'At this point, I don't know if we're going to get Terri hydrated today. I'll let you know what's going on.'

"It was the last I heard from her.

"I got home and turned on the news. The governor had been thwarted. Evidently his press conference hinting that he might take Terri into his custody telegraphed his strategy, and Felos got a restraining order against him. Who approved the order? Judge Greer.

"Several lawyers later told me that Bush, as state governor, could have gone ahead despite the restraining order, using Florida Department of Law Enforcement agents, if necessary, to remove Terri from the hospice into his custody. I don't know. What I believe is that Jeb Bush did more for our family than any of the governors of the other forty-nine states would have done. Could he have done more? Maybe. Only Governor Bush knows. But I recognize the position he was in, and I'm not bitter."

"The Story that I heard," Bob says, "is that the governor had dispatched the FDLE and they were en route to take Terri into custody—they were literally blocks away from the hospice. And Greer apparently said that if Bush allowed them to take Terri, he would issue an order to have the governor arrested by the Pinellas Park Police Department.

"And so the FDLE was called off—and that was it."

Our last chance, our last hope, was gone. The fight for Terri's life lasted fifteen years, and, even knowing the outcome, I wouldn't have given up a day of it. She died despite our efforts, but there is no doubt we did everything we could.

And as I listen to my family in preparation for writing these pages, I'm plunged back into the turmoil of those final days. But what comes to me—what salves my wounded heart—is the knowledge of how heroic Bob and Bobby and Suzanne are. Terri gave them new lives—or if not new, then different, better ones. My pride in my family exceeds any emotion I've ever felt. I feel blessed by them. I feel blessed by God.

Chapter 22

Grieving

erri Schiavo died at 9:05 on the morning of March 31, 2005. Suzanne called to tell us that Terri's two weeks of suffering had ended, that she had died. Bob and I had been expecting the news for several days, and I thought I was prepared for it. Death would end her suffering, I rationalized. She was in a better place now, and at peace. There was a measure of relief in her dying.

Still, I began to cry and couldn't stop crying. The will I had needed to keep myself available for my family—to get through the days—was no longer necessary, and I could weep for as long as I wished without regard for those around me: Bob and my brother, Mikey, who were weeping, too.

My muscles seemed to have lost their capacity to hold me up. I slumped in the backseat of Mikey's car as we drove toward the hospice, silently but gratefully accepting Bob's comforting embrace. As always, he was strong when I was at my weakest.

We stopped at the odds-and-ends shop, where we were met by David Gibbs. David was dressed in a business suit and tie, very proper and formal, once an outsider, now part of the family, who had glimpsed the depth of our pain and did all he could to alleviate it. He suggested we go right away to the hospice, and we walked outside.

Shouts. Screams. Television cameras and microphones thrust into our faces like attack birds. Police surrounded us, pushing away the crowd, but still the questions flew: "How do you feel, Mrs. Schindler?" "Anything to say, Mrs. Schindler?" "Last words for Terri, Mrs. Schindler?" As though I could talk with a voice stifled by tears.

Finally we reached the hospice entrance. Bobby and Suzanne were there, their faces white with grief. Unbelievably we were stopped and searched and made to show our ID. Finally the guards let us through, and we walked toward Terri's room for the last time. Michael Schiavo's lawyer, Deborah Bushnell, was standing at the doorway. I remember thinking she was the devil herself. I didn't see Michael or George Felos, but the hospice administrator was there, and a lot of nurses, and five or six police officers. Father Pavone was there, too, a welcome presence among the enemy.

We had to sign in again, then started to enter Terri's room. Bushnell stopped us. "Only the family," she said, and pointed to my brother. "That guy's not allowed in there."

The four of us pushed into the room. Terri was lying on the bed, still as marble.

"The scene was unforgettable," Suzanne says. "Horrible. Mom throws herself on Terri and is just incoherent, sobbing uncontrollably. There are three policemen in the room—Michael had ordered them to be with us—and one of them tries to pull her away from Terri. Dad's screaming at them to give us privacy. They're saying no. Meanwhile, Bobby turns and yells for Mikey to get into the room. And Dad's shouting, 'You let Mikey in the room. He's family!' They finally let Mikey in, but they wouldn't let him go near Terri."

Bob remembers screaming at the police to let Mikey in and give us some privacy. "I told them to get out of the room," he says, "and they refused. I said, 'For God's sake, she's dead! Do you think we're going to steal her body? Will you please have the courtesy to give us some privacy?'"

"I told Dad to forget about the policemen," Bobby continues. "I thought he was going to have a stroke. 'Tend to Mom,' I said, and Dad went over to her. And then we all sat there and things quieted down. Everyone kind of got their composure, all except Mom, who was crying—lying on Terri, hugging her, and crying hysterically, not wanting to let go."

I was holding Terri. Mikey came over and put his arms around me. "You've got to get up," he said. "You've got to get up." And Bob kept saying to my brother, "Leave her alone for a little while. Let her stay there."

So Mikey let me be for a few precious minutes more. I hugged Terri and told her good-bye. Then Mikey took my arm. I stood up and let him lead me to a chair at the foot of Terri's bed. The policeman came over and said, "You can't stay here. You can't stay here," and Bob said, "Leave her alone. She wants to sit here for a little while." The policeman said, "You cannot stay here." "That's not fair," Bob told him. "She has a right to stay here with her daughter." The policeman said, "I'm sorry. You can't stay. You have to get up." That's when I did get up and went outside in the hallway. Father Pavone was standing there giving Terri last rites. He hadn't been allowed in her room. For twelve years, Michael had been using Terri to torture us. Even at the end, he didn't stop.

I don't remember who ushered us all into a private room, probably someone from the hospice staff. We were alone with David Gibbs and Mikey.

"We never saw Michael," Suzanne says. "In the whole two weeks Terri's feeding tube was out, we never saw him. The funny thing about that is that there's only one road in and out of the hospice. And no one ever knew how he got through all the media, what car he came in. He was like a ghost."

The problem we faced was how to get out of the hospice without being trampled by the media. They knew by this time that Terri had passed, and, as Suzanne says, "they all wanted a piece of us." Bobby and Suzanne were strong enough—and angry enough at the way we were treated—to talk to them, but Bob didn't want to see them, and I was muted by anguish: the idea of the crowds outside filled me with horror.

My belief that God sends you special people when you are most in need was reinforced when in 2004 we were befriended by a group of Franciscans, members of The Franciscan Brothers of Peace out of Minnesota. Brother Paul O'Donnell, their founder, had served as our spokesperson a number of times, holding press conferences for our family. They remained at our side the whole time during and before this current crisis. They did our grocery shopping, cleaned our house, did the wash, and taxied us wherever we wished to go.

David Gibbs contacted them now and arranged to have them drive up to the hospice's rear entrance in a minivan. All Bob and I wanted to do was go home. Family and friends would be there to console us, and we could finally have the privacy denied us at the hospice.

So we left the room and walked to the side door. The van was waiting. There were news helicopters overhead. I saw police on motorcycles in front of and behind the van, an escort to lead it through the media that blocked the road to the hospice.

Bob's memory is clearest:

"All I was thinking of at the time was Princess Diana and the paparazzi. We had to go slowly because the Brothers didn't want to kill anybody. Mary had her head down on my lap, but I kept looking out. There were people running alongside the van with cameras. One guy had a camera with one of those long lenses, and *crack*, it hit the window, and Mary was startled and started to cry. The cameraman was thrown to the ground but got up and started running toward us again. I thought, *What a bunch of lowlifes. At a time like this, they'll get themselves killed trying to get a picture of a family in agony.*"

Eventually, the media stopped chasing us—there was nothing, really for them to hear or see—and we made the few miles home without more trouble. There, our extended family of brothers and sisters, uncles and aunts, cousins, nieces, and nephews welcomed us with love, and I was able to dry my tears and great them.

Getting away was harder for Suzanne and Bobby.

"We left by the front door," Bobby says, "behind four or five policemen who were pushing people out of the way so we could get to the odds-and-ends shop. Let's put it this way: the media were blocking the sun. There was one big circle of cameras around us, at least a hundred of them, and reporters with microphones and reporters with notebooks, all yelling at us, trying to get our attention.

"We didn't say anything to anybody. Suzy was holding my shoulders, kind of crouched down, and I was holding onto the cop ahead of me and he was grabbing on to the cop ahead of him, so we were a chain. I had the feeling that if the chain broke, we'd be done for. But at least we reached the shop and were able to duck inside. The police stayed outside to make sure nobody broke down the door."

"At this point we all just wanted to go home," Suzanne continues. "To Mom and Dad's house. My husband, Michael, drove up to the side of the shop. He had a black truck with tinted windows, and I ducked in next to him on the front seat and put my head down.

"Then, all of a sudden, a dozen cameras were plastered against the windows, including the windshield, and we couldn't move. I panicked. 'Drive!' I yelled to Michael, who was just a few inches away. 'I can't!' he said. 'They've blockaded the truck.' Oh, it was horrible! I was yelling at Michael, and he was screaming at the people in front of us. I felt like I was going to suffocate. At that point, the police came running over to help. They cleared some people away from the front of the truck, and Michael squealed the tires. The rest of the cameramen jumped back, and Michael drove away as fast as he could, still cursing.

"We drove to my parents' place. A lot of the family were there. Mom and Dad were walking around in a daze, but at least they were surrounded by people who loved them. It wasn't exactly peaceful—there were too many people around. Still, there was room for them to breathe. The sight of the hospital room and Terri's corpse was still in my brain. I hoped they could lose the image, if only for a few hours. Bobby wasn't there. I wondered what had happened to him."

"I waited in the odds-and-ends shop for a while," Bobby explains, "though I'm not sure why. Just wanted to be away from the family, I guess, to be alone with my own sadness. The media crowd around the shop thinned, and after about an hour, I went to get my car to drive to Mom and Dad's house. One or two people approached me. I thought they wanted an interview, so I said, 'No. I'm going home.'

"I went back to Mom and Dad's house around noon. By then, all the relatives had gathered, coming from Orlando, from Corning, from Pennsylvania. They had filled the house with food so Mom didn't have to shop. My Uncle Ed and Aunt Linda, Uncle Jack and Aunt Betty—Dad's cousins—were there. They had arrived a few days earlier to see Terri one last time. David Gibbs had called Felos to ask that they be put back on the visitors' list—Michael had removed their names 'They hadn't come in the past,' we were told was Michael's reaction. 'Why should they be included now?'

"On the drive home, I had heard President Bush's press conference when he offered condolences for Terri's death; at the house, I listened to Rush Limbaugh. He must have talked about Terri for two hours, and I remember his closing words: 'Today, America, we have hit rock bottom.' I thought so, too, and once more was filled with humility and awe. The president, who is the most powerful man in the world, and Rush Limbaugh, arguably the most powerful voice in radio: united with us, with Terri. It was beyond comprehension.

"I turned off the radio, stretched out on the floor, and fell asleep."

We knew we had to make a public statement, but were not sure how to go about it. Bob called David Gibbs, who suggested we hold a press conference at the hospice at four o'clock. Together with David, who acted as editor, we wrote a statement to be sent to the media across the world:

As you are aware, Terri is now with God and she has been released from all earthly burdens. After these recent years of neglect at the hands of those who were supposed to protect and care for her, she is finally at peace with God for eternity. We are speaking on behalf of our entire family this evening as we share some thoughts and messages to the world regarding our sister and the courageous battle that was waged to save her life from starvation and dehydration.

We have a message for the volunteers that helped our family:

Thank you for all that you've done for our family. Thank you to the hundreds of doctors who volunteered to help Terri. Thank you to the fifty doctors who provided statements under oath to help Terri. Thank you to the lawyers who stood for Terri's life in the courtrooms of our nation. From running our family's website, to driving us around, to making meals, to serving in so many ways—thank you to all of the volunteers who have been so kind to our family through all of this.

We have a message for the supporters and people praying worldwide:

Please continue to pray that God gives grace to our family as we go through this very difficult time. We know that many of you never had the privilege to personally know our wonderful sister, Terri, but we assure you that you can be proud of this remarkable woman who has captured the attention of the world. Following the example of the Lord Jesus, our family abhors any violence or any threats of violence. Threatening words dishonor our faith, our family, and our sister, Terri. We would ask that those who support our family be completely kind in their words and deeds toward others.

We have a message to the media:

We appreciate your taking Terri's case to the nation. Please afford our family privacy to grieve at this time. The patience and graciousness of the on-site media here at hospice has been deeply appreciated by our family.

We have a message to the many government officials who tried to help Terri:

Thank you for all that you've done. Our family will be forever grateful to all of the outstanding public servants who have tried to save Terri.

We have a message to all of the religious leaders who tried to help Terri:

Thank you to all people of faith who demonstrated love for Terri and strength of conviction to defend the sacredness of all human life as a precious gift from God. Our family is highly honored that the Holy Father, Pope John Paul II, would speak out so boldly on behalf of our sister, Terri.

We have a message of forgiveness:

Throughout this ordeal, we are reminded of the words of Jesus on the cross: "Father, forgive them, for they know not what they do." Our family seeks forgiveness for anything that we have done in standing for Terri's life that has not demonstrated the love and compassion required of us by our faith.

We have a message to parents worldwide:

Our family would encourage parents to spend time with their children and to cherish each and every moment of each and every day with them as a precious gift from God.

We have a message to Terri from her family:

As a member of our family unable to speak for yourself, you spoke loudly. As a member of our family unable to stand under your own power, you stood with a grace and a dignity that made your family proud. Terri, we love you dearly, but we know that God loves you more than we do. We must accept your untimely death as God's will. Terri, your life and legacy will continue to live on, as the nation is now awakened to the plight of thousands of voiceless people with disabilities that were previously unnoticed. Your family intends to stand up for the other "Terri's" around the nation and we will do all that we can to change the law so that others won't face the same fate that has befallen you.

I didn't go to the press conference. The idea of facing the public with my private grief was too much to bear. I understood the need to speak to the media, but I wanted to be Terri's mom for a little while longer. I wanted to commune with her one-on-one and let those memories come that related only to us.

So I stayed behind, with my longtime friends, Judy Bader and Fran Casler, while the others piled into cars and drove back to our headquarters at the odds-and-ends shop.

Suzanne describes what happened there:

"The media had set up a press conference area in front of the hospice. At four o'clock, Dad, Bobby, our extended family, David Gibbs, Monsignor Malanowski, the Franciscan Brothers, Father Pavone, my husband, and I left the shop and walked across the street, as usual with a police escort, but this time there was no pushing and shoving, no shouts, no frenzy.

"We faced an amazing sight: rows and rows and rows of microphones, ten times the usual number, and hundreds of cameras, their flashbulbs going off like huge fireflies. I remember standing in front of a microphone and thinking, *How am I going to get through this? I can't lose it. I can't break down.* It was eerie. My sister had died that morning, and here Dad and Bobby and I were in front of the world.

"Bobby and I had rehearsed how we would split up our family statement, and we read it without faltering. The press was very respectful. Afterwards, many people told me how moved they were, but I felt like an actor playing a part. Only when the conference was over, when we were all back in the shop, did the pain of Terri's death return."

"**Right after the conference,**" Bobby says, "**one or two of the** reporters came up to me. 'Have you heard about the pope?' they asked.

"'No. What's happened?'

"'Pope John Paul was hooked to a feeding tube today.'

"*Unbelievable.* I imagined that Terri's feeding tube had been transferred to the pope, and the image brought me close to tears. Mel Gibson's movie, *The Passion of the Christ* and Gibson's recent call offering support had moved me in the same way. After years of estrangement, I felt close to my faith, and to me the feeding tube was no coincidence, but a sign of God's acknowledgment of Terri's worth and Terri's suffering."

We believe it is no coincidence that on the very day Terri died from having food and water denied her, Pope John Paul II, her chief shepherd on earth and the man who promulgated the Gospel of Life, received a feeding tube for nutrition, hydration, and comfort. He was aware of Terri's plight and what the judicial execution by dehydration and starvation meant to the vulnerable of our world. Nor is it a coincidence that both Terri and Pope John Paul II (who passed just two days after Terri) died during the Easter season, the most holy time of the year for Catholics, representing the passion, death, and resurrection of our Lord Jesus Christ.

"Somebody told us there was going to be a memorial," Bob remembers. "A nondenominational service somewhere in Pinellas Park. Everyone was exhausted, drained. I said, 'Well, someone has to go,' and a whole bunch of fingers pointed at me.

"The memorial was in a church—for the life of me, I can't remember which one—and I went there right from the shop. It seemed like there were ten thousand people there. Even the balcony was packed. There were rabbis—one of them kissed me on the lips—black and white clergymen, two or three priests, a Muslim cleric. There was music. Catholics stood side by side with the Baptists, Methodists stood with Jews, everyone family, brought together by Terri.

"I heard people addressing the attendees. I was asked to stand, and I did, apologizing because I was wearing shorts and everybody else was dressed up. But nobody cared, and the sympathy that poured out from everyone, no matter what faith they were, or what color, or what profession, blew me away.

"I said to myself, *Now here's a miracle.*"

Many people came back to our house, but they didn't stay long. Mikey and my sister-in-law, C.B., were living with us. I assured them there was nothing more they could do for me. Bobby returned to his home, Suzanne and Michael back to their daughter.

Bob and I were alone. We didn't say much to each other—at least, I don't remember any of our words—but I was enormously grateful for his presence and his love. The world seemed hollow without Terri. Hollow and silent and sad.

I thought of the Christ welcoming her to heaven and was comforted.

On Tuesday, April 5, 2005, at seven in the evening, a funeral Mass was celebrated for Terri at the Most Holy Name of Jesus Catholic Church in Gulfport, a suburb of St. Petersburg. Monsignor Malanowski was the principal celebrant. More than eight hundred people filled the church to capacity and flowed out the doors to the adjoining courtyard. I thought it was the most beautiful of all the services for Terri. There was a calmness to it, a sense of awe. Terri was with everyone who attended.

In the days and weeks that followed, we attended Masses in Philadelphia and Jacksonville. Condolences poured in from all over the world. It became clear to us that Terri's life, her suffering and death, had touched the lives of thousands, if not millions, of people. *She belongs to them now,* I thought with a touch of regret. *We must share her.*

Chapter 23

Autopsy

*T*he services and memorials are neverending and, in fact, continue to this day. I went to several of them, always with Bob, and they brought a measure of comfort. To our amazement, people came up to ask for our autographs, as if we were celebrities. Maybe we were, but if so, it was nothing we sought and nothing we savored. We hated it.[1]

If Terri was to be remembered, we all felt, it would not be because we were on television or in someone's autograph book, and it wouldn't be through commemorations and sermons. We needed something solid to honor her memory.

So we decided to restructure the foundation we established in 2001 and use it for a vehicle for helping people with disabled daughters, sons, husbands, wives, or grandparents cope with their problem more knowledgeably, and therefore more effectively, than we did. We had had no tools. We would supply others with one.

To put a mother—to put anyone—through what Terri and my family went through, and to see hospitals, hospices, and courts do something so cruel to another human being that should never ever have been done, is beyond my understanding. You don't dehydrate or starve somebody to death. Not here. Not in America. Not

---

[1] It continues to happen, virtually every day. But all we did was fight for our daughter's life. Why does that make us celebrities?

anywhere. But to do it, and *knowingly* do it, is something I will never forget, and something no other mother should have to see. As David Gibbs said, "You can't starve a dog that way; you can't starve a mass murderer that way; the Geneva Convention keeps us from starving prisoners that way—but they did it that way to Terri."

So my own motive was clear: I determined to devote my life to making sure that what happened to me and my child would never have to happen again.

Actually Terri didn't die from starvation—she died from dehydration. The autopsy on Terri's body was conducted by Dr. Jon R. Thogmartin, chief medical examiner for Pasco and Pinellas Counties (the Sixth Circuit).[2] His report was issued on June 15, 2005. It included analyses by a variety of medical experts—a neuropathologist, an anatomic/clinical/forensic pathologist, a toxicologist, and a radiologist. Eighty-six X-rays were taken and 188 photos of her body. There's no question that the report was thorough.

The media leaped on the autopsy report like lions. Terri was "brain-dead," they said. She was in a persistent vegetative state and had been for years. She was blind at the moment of her death. She couldn't swallow.

The media verdict, almost universally proclaimed: it was a blessing that Terri had died; it made no sense to keep her alive any longer. But a close reading of the report shows that this conclusion was not nearly as absolute as the media made it out to be—that, indeed, the report is full of ambiguities and unanswered questions.

---

[2] Our request for a neutral pathologist or a neutral observer was turned down.

For example, while it is incontestably true that Terri was severely brain-injured, that does *not* mean she was brain-dead or even PVS. The distinction is vital. To Barbara Weller, a Florida-certified attorney and a colleague of David Gibbs, there was no question that Terri was responsive, even at the end.

Barbara visited Terri three times between December 2004 and March 2005, the last on the day the feeding tube was removed. (As our lead attorneys, she, Pat Anderson, and David Gibbs were allowed on the visitors' list, while Tom Broderson was taken off.) She wrote extensive descriptions of all three visits. Here's an excerpt from the last. Suzanne was in the room with her when the events she describes happened, and verifies them:

> Terri was sitting in her lounge chair and her aunt[3] was sitting at the foot of the chair. I stood up and leaned over Terri. I took her arms in both of my hands. I said to her, "Terri, if you could only say, 'I want to live.' This whole thing would be over today." I begged her to try very hard to say, "I want to live." To my enormous shock and surprise, Terri's eyes opened wide, she looked at me square in the face, and with a look of great concentration, she said, "Ahhhhhh."
>
> Then, seeming to summon up all the strength she had, she virtually screamed "Waaaaaaaa." She yelled so loudly that Michael Vitadamo, Terri's sister Suzanne's husband, and the female police officer who were standing together outside Terri's door clearly heard her. At that point, Terri had a look of anguish on her face that I had never seen before and she seemed to be struggling hard but was unable to complete the sentence. She became very frustrated and began to cry. I was horrified that I was causing Terri so much anguish. Suzanne and I began to stroke Terri's face and hair to comfort her. I

---

[3]   Mikey's wife, C.B.

told Terri I was very sorry. It had not been my intention to upset her so much. Suzanne and I assured Terri that her efforts were much appreciated and that she did not need to say anything more. I promised Terri I would tell the world that she had tried to say, "I want to live."

Almost immediately, doctors began to refute the press analysis of the report. Thomas W. Hejkal, MD, PhD, Associate Professor, Department of Ophthalmology at the Nebraska Medical Center, said that although the autopsy findings certainly indicated that Terri had some deficit in her visual field, "cortical blindness could only be diagnosed by assessing her visual function while she was living." Dr. Bernadine Healy, a former director of the National Institutes of Health, pointed out that an autopsy can tell us nothing about Terri's neurological function. Dr. Michael DeGeorgia, head of the neurology/neurosurgery intensive-care unit at the Cleveland Clinic Foundation, said that the PVS diagnosis "cannot be confirmed by surgery." Dr. Mack Jones, a Florida neurologist, noted that while there was evidence of severe brain injury, "these findings, nor any other findings have no bearing on the diagnosis of 'minimal consciousness' or PVS." Dr. William Cheshire, the neurologist from the Mayo Clinic, agreed with our position that Terri was awake, aware, and at least minimally cognitive, and quickly made his opinion known to Governor Bush. And Harvard neuropathologist E. Tessa Hedley White said that a pathologic examination of the brain "can't tell if there is a persistent vegetative state or not."

Even Dr. Thogmartin wrote that "PVS is a clinical diagnosis arrived at through physical examination of living patients. By definition, an autopsy is performed after a patient dies." As Diana Lynne points out in her excellent book, *Terri's Story*, Dr. Stephen

Nelson, a consulting pathologist, who helped Thogmartin with the autopsy report, admitted that while Terri's symptoms were consistent with PVS, he could not rule out the possibility that Terri was in a minimally conscious state. And Thogmartin conceded that it couldn't be determined how much Terri's long period of dehydration contributed to the shrinkage of her brain.

"Mrs. Schiavo's heart was anatomically normal without any areas of recent or remote myocardial infarction," Dr. Thogmartin noted. "An underlying, undiagnosed cardiac anomaly is possible, but diagnostics at the time [the time of her collapse] along with postmortem examination of the heart were negative."

Translation: A heart attack wasn't the cause of Terri's collapse.

Nor was bulimia nervosa. "According to those that knew Mrs. Schiavo," Dr. Thogmartin wrote, "her eating and drinking habits included eating lots of salads, eating a large omelet on weekends and drinking large amounts of ice tea. No one observed Mrs. Schiavo taking diet pills, binging and purging, or consuming laxatives, and she apparently never confessed to her family or friends about having an eating disorder. Recent interviews with family members, physicians, and coworkers revealed no additional information supporting the diagnosis of bulimia nervosa and, indeed, other signs and symptoms of bulimia nervosa were not reported to be present."

The main argument *for* bulimia that Michael Schiavo's lawyers used when he sued her ob-gyn and family doctor for malpractice in 1992, was knocked down by Dr. Thogmartin's findings:

On February 25, 1990, according to available records, a 911 call was made at approximately 0540 hrs.[4] Both Mr. Schiavo and Bobby Schindler were present prior to arrival of emergency responders. They both describe her as lying prone and breathing, or at least they describe her as "making gurgling noises." According to her medical records, paramedics began treating Mrs. Schiavo at 0552 hrs. The Pinellas County EMS report records her as supine in the hallway with no respiration and her initial cardiac rhythm was ventricular fibrillation ... Her time of arrival at Humana Hospital-Northside was 0646 hrs. At 0701 hrs, her blood was drawn and that sample showed hypokalemia [low potassium] ... one hour after her initial collapse and after over 30 minutes of CPR ... Her doctors began potassium supplementation almost immediately resulting in a rapid rise of her potassium ... She also received epinephrine [from the EMS] ... The dosage of epinephrine she received was sufficient to cause ... lowering of potassium ... Thus it is reasonable to conclude that Mrs. Schiavo's level ... measured after a period of ventricular fibrillation, epinephrine, and fluid administration was an unreliable measure of her pre-arrest potassium level. Thus, the main piece of evidence supporting a diagnosis of bulimia nervosa is suspect.

It is unlikely that Michael will repay the doctors the money he won from them in the malpractice suit.

---

[4] Michael told Larry King that Terri collapsed at 4:30, and he confirmed the time to the medical examiner. The seventy-minute time lapse, as Mark Fuhrman writes in *Silent Witness*, is highly suspicious, pointing to a scenario that Michael and Terri fought, that Michael inadvertently got her in a stranglehold—a position that might not leave marks on her neck—and that she collapsed because oxygen could not reach her brain. The autopsy report confirmed Fuhrman's theory that they would not find any signs of trauma to her neck just as when she was initially examined at Humana Northside.

❧

We knew that Terri was visually impaired, but our attorneys and other witnesses, like Father Pavone, saw her recognize us until near the end. My guess is that severe dehydration caused her blindness, as it caused the shrinkage of her brain, another reason why starvation and dehydration are such cruel means for ending a life.

As for her inability to swallow, this seems true at the time of her death, but not necessarily during the course of her life. Swallowing can be helped by rehabilitation. So can movement, cognizance, and speech. Our great bitterness throughout these thirteen years was that Michael stopped rehabilitation when it could so easily have been granted. The autopsy report brought home the full extent of how far Terri had disintegrated. But she had not disappeared, had years of life ahead of her. She had our love and her God on her side. We would have kept her safe.

Shortly after the autopsy report was released, Father Pavone put it in its spiritual perspective:

The autopsy goes on to say that Terri's brain was "profoundly atrophied" and only half the normal size. Fine. If that's what the experts tell us, there is no problem believing them. But what does that mean, that she was only half human, only half a person, or that she had only half the rights the rest of us have? That is the conclusion we must never accept. That is a conclusion that does not come from autopsy but from a callous disregard for human life. Terri did not die from atrophy of the brain. She died from atrophy of compassion. Too many people, starting with Michael, were unwilling to accept the fact that profoundly injured people require profound compassion and care. Even if the autopsy report showed that Terri was ten times more damaged than she was, our moral obligation to respect and protect her life would not change at all. We don't have to pass a test to qualify for our human rights. An autopsy is a measure of physical damage, not of human rights.

The autopsy says Terri was blind. That is not the morally relevant point. The point is that we are blind—blind too often to the fact that even the disabled and the severely injured have the same dignity and worth as the rest of us, and show forth the image and glory of God even in their brokenness.

And oh, if Michael had only let us rehabilitate her! I grieve now less for her death than for how far she might have come.

Chapter 24

Terri's Legacy

*T*hrough Terri's death, we've learned the value of life. Not only the life that most of us enjoy—bodies healthy, minds alert, the capacity to love intact, able to reach out to our neighbors and our God—but the life that was Terri's: limited, disabled, precarious, confined to a bed or a wheelchair, unable to eat by herself, dress herself, speak for herself, yet limitlessly precious. Injury or disability does not mitigate a human being's capacity to love or to receive love. Mother Teresa said, "We are made to love and be loved."

All life is sacred. This is a seemingly simple concept. It's the basic moral underpinning of most religions. Bob and I were brought up on the idea, and we passed it on to our children. Until Terri's collapse, we didn't think much about it; it was a given. But since Terri fell, we think about it every day—what it *really* means, and why it is fundamental to how we live out each day.

"I think that as a nation, a society, we've lost sight of the value of all human life," Bobby says. "And now we're deciding who should live and who should die, based on their disability and, in Terri's case, depending on how profoundly brain-injured they are. We look at people like Terri as nonpersons, as having less value, less worth, than so-called normal people.

"It's relatively simple now to kill someone based on two criteria: Is the person PVS? Is it the person's wish that he or she die? Our laws—and they're only two decades old—make taking a life like Terri's easy. One of the goals of the Terri Schindler Schiavo Foundation is to make sure we elect legislators and judges who will change the laws to give protection to the disabled and vulnerable. Another is to help the disabled directly, both through counseling and through active intervention. We've already been successful in preventing the premature death of a few individuals, who are now recovering! People contact us daily and we give them suggestions: the names of lawyers in their community who will fight to keep their loved ones alive; the lessons we learned in fighting for Terri. We've had attorneys from around the country willing to donate their time and their skill. Doctors and therapists from around the country have volunteered. The response has been overwhelming. Groups in America, Germany, Ireland, and New Zealand have invited us to speak on right-to-life and disability issues.

"It all makes us believe that the foundation is a worthy endeavor. What we are doing is right. It's what Terri would have expected of us."

Here, Bobby speaks for all of us:

"People have to make the distinction between what's legal and what's moral. Just because we're legally allowed to starve someone to death doesn't make it morally right. It's basic to our religion that taking any innocent life is wrong, and the foundation is established in Terri's name to help prevent this from happening to anyone else.

"We need to be clear that this isn't about so-called end-of-life issues. What we're talking about is the intentional killing of innocent, vulnerable people who can't speak for themselves and have been labeled as 'unworthy of life' or who are deemed 'unwanted.'

"There is not now and never has been a 'right' to die. There is no 'right' to suicide. This is because there is no right to *absolute* personal autonomy. We have obligations to each other and to God. And no one can claim for themselves a 'right' to deny the value or worth of another human being's life. We all have a *right to life*, and it is given by God. It is a gift."

"I think Terri was selected by God as a messenger," Bob says. "What happened to Terri is happening throughout the country and in different parts of the world. I came to grips with it at a point just before her feeding tube was removed for the last time. There was nothing we could do any longer, I realized. We had the best attorneys, the support of millions, media attention for Terri's cause. And we got absolutely nowhere.

"That's when I turned to God. I said, 'Okay, if You're going to allow Terri to die, and it's pretty obvious to me that You are, then You want to use Terri to get the word out, as a messenger.' That's how I viewed it.

"And, even after death, Terri's done God's work and continues to do it. Thousands of people drew up wills to live—wills that said they wanted to live—because of Terri. Thousands of people realized they're mortal or in danger of sudden disability, and they've made preparations. Thousands of people realized that the judicial system thinks of killing people like Terri as justifiable homicide. Thousands of people now know about futile care committees and the bias against the severely disabled by the medical and insurance companies; or if they don't, our goal is to let them know.

"A major objective of the foundation is to establish task forces throughout the country, so that when there's a patient like Terri, or a hospital says, 'We're going to have to disconnect,' or they recommend the taking of a loved one's life, there will be someone on hand to advise the caregiver.

"Life support's not just about respirators and other machinery. It's about spiritual support, and it means fighting back against doctors and hospitals who say—as a doctor did about my mother— 'She's led a good life. Let her go.'"

Bobby, too, has a long-range goal.

"I'd love to open up a Terri Schindler Schiavo care center. Where people could bring someone like Terri and not have to worry about *their* lives being in jeopardy. A safe haven, fully staffed, where the patients are treated like human beings. And if that works, we could establish havens across the country—in every state in the land."

I hear these plans, and they fill me with hope. Bobby is a changed person. He tells me he wakes up every morning with a sense of purpose and excitement, a feeling that he is doing God's work—and Terri's.

"I've never been so passionate about what I'm doing in life," he says. "I feel like I'm trying to make a difference in our world. I think Terri has blazed a way for us.

"We deal with life and death every day at the foundation. Everything starts with life and death. And we're out there on the front lines trying to do something to help people. All this came from Terri. And, God willing, I hope I can do this the rest of my life.

"They talked about Terri having no value in our society, that she should be dead because she has no worth. But look what she's done! She's touched millions of people around the world. Christ works through the most vulnerable and the most sick. And I think this is a perfect example of Him using Terri—being the most vulnerable and sick—and how she's been able to change the world from a position of complete vulnerability. As evil as her killing was, we can also look at the good that's eventually going to come from it."

Suzanne, like Bobby, is tirelessly going around the country speaking on right-to-life and disability issues and telling Terri's story with a compassion that seems to draw her audiences in. Her first priority, though, is her daughter, Alex. Suzanne was shunned by her parish after Terri's feeding tube was removed, and not once did Alex's priest talk to Alex or to Suzanne. The only time anyone made an effort to help Alex was when she had a breakdown in class, and her guidance counselor took her to church to light a candle for Terri. Alex is now in sixth grade and thriving. Sometimes Suzanne brings her to the office after school, and her presence is sunlight.

Bob remains my strength, my mainstay. He is deeply involved in the day-to-day operation of the foundation, travels across the country to give talks about Terri and the judicial system he believes failed her, and continues to search for the facts surrounding Terri's collapse. I worry that he works too hard, but when he's teasing Bobby or Suzanne, I see in him the young father of our children, and my worry eases.

As for me, I am holding true to my promise to try to make sure that what happened to Terri will never happen again. The foundation is my best tool. I'm in the office every day that I'm not out on speaking engagements, answering emails from those seeking advice, trying to comfort and console, giving, as best I can, practical and spiritual help. I am more committed to my work than any I've done in the past. My days are full and rewarding, my family is around me, and Terri's spirit is in everything I do.

Terri, I realize, has drawn us together as a family. We are united in our work. We are united in our love.

When somebody you love dies, you don't get over it. People tell me you get used to it. As the years go by, you don't miss your loved one as acutely, and the pain recedes. As I write this, it's been less than a year since Terri died, so the pain is still raw. It is for all of us. I don't know what I'll be feeling in five years or ten. Right now I feel that there'll never be closure (hateful word!) and I'll never get over Terri's death.

When someone dies, it's usually from old age or sickness or a sudden, terrible accident. Terri's death was different. Terri didn't have to die, yet she died a horrible, horrible death—I can't get the images out of my mind. She was being killed over the course of thirteen years, beginning when Michael denied her rehabilitation and ending when the courts pulled out her feeding tube. We watched her needless degeneration, as others watch the ravages of old age or a slow but inevitable cancer. But Terri was young and didn't have cancer. We were forced to watch her being murdered.

"How does a parent ever get over something like that?" Suzanne, herself a parent, asks. "When I look at Mom and Dad, I see Laci Peterson's mother and know how she felt. At least with her, she didn't have to watch it happen. Scott Peterson is on death row, which has to bring some sense of justice to Laci's parents. Maybe they can sleep a little better. But Terri's murderers are free. For thirteen years, we watched her being killed and were ultimately powerless to stop it despite the strongest allies imaginable.

"I'm fortunate because my daughter Alex is a gem. I want to be an example of happiness for her, and I want her to be happy, although realistic, too. She knows what happened to Terri and experienced the pain as well. But I don't want her to dwell on it. I want her to have some sense of normalcy. And I don't want to walk around miserable and depressed because of it. I don't think Terri would want that. Our lives are so short.

"I'm so proud of Terri. I'll never make the impact she made. Everyone knows the name Terri Schiavo, and everybody knows about her fight for life. It's incredible.

"We believe that Terri's life was worth fighting for, and we've never wavered in our commitment, even when people said, 'Let her go.' When the autopsy report came out, it simply confirmed that we had done the right thing. She was our flesh and blood.

"It really makes you dig down and question yourself on whether you'd have done the same thing for someone you never even knew. I think I would. I think all of us would. That's what we're doing now."

It says in the Scriptures that God will not be mocked," Bobby says. "I think what they did to Terri was mocking God, and that He'll hold people accountable for what they did to Terri.

"I pray to God to help me find forgiveness for Michael and Felos. And I ask Him to help my parents to get over their anger and forgive them, too. It takes the grace of God. I don't see how they can do it on their own.

"Am I there yet? I don't know. I don't think there's one day when you can say you've reached forgiveness. But my relationship with Christ has helped me through this time. Jesus says it's easy to love those who love us back. The challenge is to love and forgive those who are our enemies. People tell me all the time, 'You need to pray for Michael. You need to pray and find forgiveness for him.' To live in Christ we have to forgive. Our relationship with Christ is the only thing that matters. But it's difficult. Extremely difficult."

"I don't know that I could ever forgive," Bob says. "I also pray that one day I'll be able to. But I have too much anger at what's happened. It would be helpful for me to see the people who murdered Terri exposed and put behind bars. Then I'd feel at least some justice was done, and maybe I could deal with Terri's death better. But right now I feel it was judicial homicide and that these people should be punished for what they've done. They should be in jail. Until that happens, I don't see myself in any way forgiving or forgetting. And I will spend every ounce of energy I have to see that they are exposed.

"We made a commitment to Terri that we would do everything within our power to get her rehabilitated and help her recover. We failed. Our new commitment is to people like Terri. We will do everything we can to protect them, and this time, God willing, we will not fail."

I share Bob's anger, of course, but I don't hate Felos and I don't hate Michael. Forgive them? No, I'm not there yet. I'm not built up with rage, but I'm not at peace, either. Every day I pray that God helps me a little more toward forgiving them. Hopefully, with the help of God, maybe someday I can.

Sometimes when I'm on television or speaking on the radio, I tell myself, *Don't cry.* My tears are private. People say, 'You don't seem to have much emotion,' but no one knows what I go through when I have a quiet moment alone, or if I'm in church. That's when I cry. I think about Terri and cry.

Every single morning when I wake up I say good morning to her. Every single morning. After that, she's never really out of my mind.

The Terri Schindler Schiavo Foundation has two rooms and a bathroom. In the back room are our desks, our files, our computers, a coffeemaker, a refrigerator, a television set, and, in an alcove, a conference table and chairs. It looks like any office—we could be accountants or bookies.

The front room, though it, too, has desks and computers, is a kind of shrine to Terri. There is a picture of us being greeted by the pope in 2005, several Defender of Life Awards, and two yellow construction helmets signed by members of the media after some of their television light stands had fallen on Bobby and Suzanne in front of the hospice on a windy night. But mostly there are artifacts I associate with Terri, among them a drawing of Terri being embraced by Jesus; the front page of the *Tampa Tribune* announcing Terri's death; a drawing of the *Pietà*; a poem entitled "Why Did Terri Die?"; a quilt with a picture of an angel blessing two children in its center, surrounded by handwritten quotes from the Bible, one of them reading, "For I will restore health to you and heal you of your wounds, says the Lord" (Jeremiah 30:17); a drawing by Terri of a dog and a butterfly; a superb painting of Terri herself; a painting of a cross festooned with flowers; a picture of

Mother Teresa; several small statues, including one of the Virgin Mary holding the infant Jesus; a particularly moving drawing of Christ.

I love that room. In the last days of Terri's life, when reporters were hounding us outside of hospice, when it was literally unsafe to go outside our own apartment, when every news channel blared Terri's name and red-faced pundits screamed at each other about euthanasia and the so-called right-to-die, when we were the focus of a million people and the subject of a million arguments, I remember thinking, *Terri's lost. No one knows her. No one cares about her, only what she stands for. She's not flesh and blood anymore. She's an icon.*

I felt lost, too, separated from Terri by a sea of humanity. When I visited her toward the end, there was always a policeman in the room. When I held her, even when she smiled back at me or seemed comforted by my presence, I still felt I'd lost her and she'd lost me.

But here in the front room of the foundation, surrounded by pictures and memories, I feel I'm close to her, that I've found her again. Terri. A normal girl from an ordinary family. Lost and found.

Epilogue:
A Lesson for Us All

*T*erri's tragic and needless death, and her life as a disabled woman, have forced us as a society to confront our prejudice against the disabled.

Are we going to love and care for our weak and vulnerable brothers and sisters? Are we willing to say to them, "You may be injured, weak, or dependent, but your life is a gift from God to all of us"? Are we willing to see the profoundly disabled as our teachers— teaching us how to love, a lesson by which every one of us will someday be judged?

Or are we going to throw them in the trash like damaged goods?

We are Terri's family. It was natural for us to want to care for her. We loved her as a child, we loved her as an adult, and we loved her in her disability. Our love and commitment to her never changed. To us, she did not die when her brain was injured. She never left this world until she was torn from it by those who deemed her unworthy of life. We kept our promise to her: we fought for her life with all our strength.

Terri's brutal death, a legally sanctioned killing of an innocent, disabled person, revealed in the most glaring way the face of the so-called right-to-die agenda, an agenda which pervades the medical industry.

The diagnosis of persistent vegetative state was invented by proponents of euthanasia within the medical industry to dehumanize the severely brain-injured, making it easier to kill them. This medical diagnosis is now a legally recognized term. Under Florida law, the definition of "persistent vegetative state"[1] is a permanent and irreversible condition of unconsciousness in which there is: (a) the absence of voluntary or cognitive behavior of any kind and (b) an inability to communicate or interact purposefully with the environment.

This definition means a death sentence for people with severe disabilities like Terri. There is clearly no other reason for the PVS diagnosis. Doctors and hospitals can use it to terminate a life—and even if the person is arguably *not* PVS, like Terri, there may be no way of counteracting it.

The Nazis had something called the T-4 program, devoted to eliminating all the disabled people of Germany. Hospitals and doctors were given the authority to kill those deemed "imperfect" or "undesirable." Well, it's happening here in America.

As Bobby says, "The term 'vegetative state' makes me furious. People don't describe them as a disabled person anymore, but as vegetables. In fact, I read about a kid in college who dressed as a vegetable for Halloween and called herself Terri Schiavo. I think 'vegetable' is used purposely. It's easier for people to rationalize taking a human life if she's in a 'vegetative state.'

"We fell into that trap ourselves. We had to argue that Terri wasn't PVS—even though she didn't fall into the PVS criteria—

---

[1] According to the *British Medical Journal*, it is misdiagnosed 43 percent of the time.

because only then would she be allowed to live. But why did Terri have to prove anything? She was a human being.

"And even if they claim someone is PVS, does that mean she's not allowed to practice her religion? Not allowed to have people she loves or who love her take care of her? Not allowed to eat and drink? Not allowed care?

"Michael claims that Terri's death by starvation and dehydration was 'peaceful and painless.' His attorney agreed, and so did some doctors. Yet most doctors say just the opposite—that dying this way is agonizing—and we saw how horrible Terri's death was. The fact is that doctors don't know, and neither do attorneys.

"But Kate does.

"Like Terri, Kate Adamson had her feeding tube removed and went without food or water for a week. Pictures of Kate in this period showed a woman suffering terribly. But unlike Michael, Kate's husband fought against Kate's doctors, finally convincing them that his wife deserved life. Kate has since improved and now speaks out about her experience, what it's like to go without food and water.[2] There's no doubt that Terri suffered just as Kate did—and God have mercy on us as a society for allowing it to happen.

"Remember, most hospitals and many doctors *want you to die.* It's convenient that way and much less expensive. Hospitals need the space, doctors need the time, and insurance companies want to hold on to their money. The profoundly disabled? Well, they're a burden, less than human. They should be 'mercifully' put away.

---

[2] www.katesjourney.com

Yet there are thousands of people near death who have gotten better. And there have been thousands of people who've thought of committing suicide only to change their minds.

Many people believe that a living will or some form of advanced health care directive is the answer to the tragedies in life such as Terri suffered. The secular media, which consistently wrote of Terri's plight as an "end-of-life issue," which it was not, advised everybody to run out to create living wills. However, living wills are increasingly unenforceable. "Futile care committees" in medical facilities across the country are overriding them every day.

Even so, a more effective route to pursue regarding your health care wishes is to grant a reliable person—preferably not a spouse or loved one, who might be too emotionally involved—a health care power of attorney. A formal "will to live" is espoused by the National Right to Life Committee and the National Euthanasia Task Force. We encourage you to contact our foundation to obtain more information.

Appendix A

Terri Schiavo
Life & Hope Network

Formerly Terri Schindler Schiavo Foundation

The Terri Schiavo Life & Hope Network is fighting for the rights of the severely disabled. We've been contacted by parents and other family members who have brought us persons like Terri—in worse shape than Terri—and are horrified at what the courts are doing. They're afraid because if they die, or are otherwise unable to care for their loved ones, judicial murder might loom.

We are dedicated:

- To advocate for persons in danger of being killed by euthanasia.

- To promote legislation that will protect the right to life and basic care of disabled and vulnerable persons. This will include efforts to reestablish food and hydration as ordinary care and not "medical treatment" as it is now defined by some in the medical and legal professions.

- To confront the culture of death in our society by establishing a grassroots volunteer network to help us speak out against the deliberate killing of the disabled or anyone deemed "unworthy" of life. This will include educational efforts to inform people about the dangers of "living wills," and the necessity for a reliable health care power of attorney to defend those in danger of not receiving the health care that is their right.

- To establish a sanctuary—a "safe haven"—where severely disabled persons, the brain injured or those classified as PVS, can live, immersed in loving care, dignity and safety. They would be afforded the best medicine, therapy and comfort that modern technology has to offer, at no cost to them or their families.

- To advance the Gospel of Life in honor of the life and legacy of Terri Schindler Schiavo.

We pray that Terri's Life & Hope Network will save the lives of other innocents. May our efforts help build a society that holds every life as sacred and worthy of our love and care. Terri's great sacrifice was not in vain. She touched the lives of millions of people throughout the world. Truly, hers was a life that matters.

Terri Schiavo Life & Hope Network

P.O. Box 521
Narberth, PA 19072
1-855-300-HOPE (4673)
info@lifeandhope.com

LifeandHope.com

In 2011, the Terri Schindler Schiavo Foundation relocated its headquarters to the Philadelphia area and changed its name.

But when the Son of Man comes in His Glory, and all angels with Him, then He will sit on His glorious throne.

All the nations will be gathered before Him; and He will separate them from one another, as the shepherd separates the sheep from the goats; and He will put the sheep on His right. And the goats on the left.

Then the King will say to those on His right, "Come, you who are blessed of My Father, inherit the kingdom prepared for you from the foundation of the world.

For I was hungry, and you gave Me something to eat;
I was thirsty, and you gave Me something to drink;
I was a stranger, and you invited Me in;
Naked, and you clothed Me;
I was sick, and you visited Me;
I was in prison, and you came to Me."

Then the righteous will answer Him, "Lord, when did we see You hungry, and feed You, or thirsty, and give You something to drink?

And when did we see You a stranger, and invite You in, or naked, and clothe You?

When did we see You sick, or in prison, and come to You?"

The King will answer and say to them, "Truly I say to you, to the extent that you did it to one of these brothers and sisters of Mine, even the least of them, you did it to Me."

Matthew 25: 31-40

Appendix B

The Affidavits

Over the course of Terri's case, numerous affidavits and statements were submitted to Judge Greer in opposition to his ruling to stop Terri's feeding and hydration, a decision he claimed was based on valid medical evidence. He paid little or no attention to them.

When the videotapes showing Terri responding were aired by the media throughout the country, they attracted the attention of hundreds of physicians and caretakers many of whom contacted Terri's attorneys with affidavits that disputed the court's neurological findings and recommended therapy and additional testing. Even these failed to sway Judge Greer.

In addition, the media neglected to report the existence of the medical affidavits and the important role these documents played in influencing Congress and the Florida Legislature to act on Terri's behalf.

Forty medical professionals submitted sworn testimony. Five full affidavits are included here. The rest can be found on Terri's website.

Declaration of Rodney Dunaway, M.D.

I, Rodney Dunaway, M.D., have personal knowledge of the facts stated in this declaration and, if called as a witness, I could and would testify competently thereto under oath. I declare as follows:

1. I am a Board Certified Neurologist. I trained at Walter Reed during the height of the Vietnam war. In the course of that experience, I saw literally hundreds of brain-injured young men. I was the Assistant Chief of Neurology at Wilford Hall USAF Medical Center in San Antonio. I was Consultant in Neurology to the NASA Flight Surgeon during some of the Apollo missions. I entered private practice in Neurology in 1971. I was Chief of Neurology at Florida Hospital Orlando for many years. I have experience with cases of brain death and vegetative state, as has *every* neurologist in practice for many years.

2. I have carefully viewed the public tapes of Terri Schiavo. It is apparent that while severely disabled, she is not brain dead, she tracks objects, she smiles. I did not see any "primitive reflexes." It appears to me that she reacts to stimuli.

3. I have been informed of the diagnostic studies upon which the decision to terminate her life have been based. It is my opinion that these studies were inadequate, and insufficient to allow a reasoned opinion by her physicians. In my opinion, further neurologic studies are needed before a declaration of Persistent Vegetative State can be made.

4. Many medical advances have been made in the area of Neuro-rehabilitation. One distinguished Neurologist has announced on television that he believes she can be rehabilitated. Mrs. Schiavo has not had the benefit of these new techniques. I submit that she should be given the chance.

5. I feel it a grave mistake to give full credence to a statement made in a conversation after watching a movie. (I hope I am not held to statements I made at age 20.)

6. I urge you, before it is too late, to provide basic nutrition to Mrs. Schiavo. If she is to be killed, pass a law dealing with the matter of Euthanasia and Assisted Suicide. Even convicted murderers sentenced to death are treated more humanely than this poor woman.

7. I declare under the penalty of perjury under the laws of the State of Florida that the foregoing is true and correct.

Executed this 23rd day of March 2005, in Longwood, Florida.

[signed by Rodney Dunaway, MD], Declarant

Declaration of Lawrence Huntoon, M.D.

I, Lawrence Huntoon, M.D., have personal knowledge of the facts stated in this declaration and, if called as a witness, I could and would testify competently thereto under oath. I declare as follows:

1. I am a medical doctor specializing in neurology in New York. I currently operate a clinical office in Derby, New York.

2. I am a Board Certified Fellow of the American Academy of Neurology. I currently serve as Editor-in-Chief of the Journal of American Physicians and Surgeons. I am also a member of the Association of American Physicians and Surgeons.

3. I have attached a copy of my curriculum vitae.

4. Although I have not physically examined Theresa Marie Schiavo, I have viewed the short video clips on Terri Schiavo's website. Based on those short video clips there appears to be evidence that Ms. Schiavo responds to her mother and is able to distinguish her mother from other persons who interact with her. There is also evidence of sustained visual pursuit, which is the clip where she is following the balloon. These behaviors indicate awareness of the environment, and this type of behavior distinguishes minimally conscious state (MCS) from persistent vegetative state (PVS).

5. The definition and diagnostic criteria for minimally conscious state were published in *Neurology,* in February 2002. Among the purposeful behavior cited in that article, which generally supports a diagnosis of MCS, is "appropriate smiling or crying in response to the linguistic or visual content of emotional but not to neutral topics or stimuli."

6. The video clips on Ms. Schiavo's website show clearly that she smiles. Her face "lights up" when her mother is talking to her. That same type of reaction does not occur when a male health care worker is talking to her. That suggests that Ms. Schiavo is able to distinguish who is talking to her and she has an appropriate "happy" response to her mother talking to her. This single behavior, according to the article cited, would be sufficient to qualify Ms. Schiavo for a diagnosis of MCS, made by an examining neurologist.

7. If there is any question about clinical interpretation of behavior (i.e. is it "reflexive" or "responsive"), then other objective, supportive testing might be considered. Although this testing is still in its infancy, there is evidence that some MCS patients retain cognitive function despite inability to communicate or follow commands. A *Neurology* article in February of 2005 cited, "These findings of active cortical networks that serve language functions suggest that some MCS patients may retain widely distributed cortical systems with potential for cognitive and sensory function despite their inability to follow simple instructions or communicate reliably."

8. Swallowing therapy, via a qualified speech therapist, should absolutely be provided in the case where artificial nutrition has been given and the artificial nutrition is being terminated. A speech therapist can provide advice on amounts and consistency of food that will minimize the risk of aspiration.

9. Food and water should be offered to patients in the ordinary way in the case where artificial nutrition and hydration are being terminated. Providing food and water in the natural way, by mouth, constitutes "ordinary care" not "treatment." Ordinary, comfort care

should always be provided irrespective of instructions regarding "limitation of treatment."

10. I would be willing to participate in the matter concerning Terri Schiavo in any way that would be helpful.

I declare under the penalty of perjury under the laws of the State of New York that the foregoing is true and correct.

Executed this 3rd day of March 2005, in Eden, New York.

[signed by Lawrence Huntoon, M.D.], Declarant

Declaration of Jacob Green, M.D., Ph.d.

I, Jacob Green, have personal knowledge of the facts stated in this declaration and, if called as a witness, I could and would testify competently thereto under oath. I declare as follows:

1. I am a medical doctor specializing in neurology in Jacksonville, Florida, practicing at Southeastern Neuroscience Institute, P.A.

2. I have been in practice as a physician for 38 years and am certified by the American Board of Psychiatry and Neurology. I hold a Ph.D. as well as an M.D. degree, and I did post-graduate residencies in both neurology and neurological surgery at the University of Alabama Hospital at Birmingham, as well as a residency in neurology at the Medical University of South Carolina Medical Center. Presently, I am or have been licensed to practice medicine in Florida, Alabama, Georgia, Virginia, and Kentucky. I have published six textbooks and more than sixty papers published in various peer-reviewed journals.

3. Although I have not physically examined Theresa Marie Schiavo, I base my opinions about her condition on a review of her medical records and on scrutiny of a videotape of the patient, dated January 22, 2000.

4. Ms. Schiavo is not in a persistent vegetative state. Based on the fact that Ms. Schiavo can look around, smile, and make verbalizations, it is my opinion that she is not in a persistent vegetative state.

5. Since the time of the original court's ruling in the Terri Schiavo matter, a new neurologic entity has, subsequently, been defined. This entity is known as "minimally conscious state" (MCS). The American Academy of Neurology's own journal has published four articles on this condition in the last several months.

6. This new diagnostic brain-damaged category clearly indicates that Terri Schiavo should be re-evaluated for the correct diagnosis (MCS).

7. Based upon my medical experience and review of the information available in this matter regarding Terri Schiavo, it is my professional opinion that the correct diagnosis for Terri is, in fact, minimally conscious state and not persistent vegetative state.

8. Since the court previously ruled that Terri is in a persistent vegetative state, new technology has become available to more accurately diagnose the current mental functioning of a patient. This new technology, which is called functional magnetic resonance imaging, or fMRI, can measure brain activity by creating multidimensional images of blood flow to various parts of the activated brain. For the first time, doctors using the MRI may predict a patient's capability for emerging or recovering from those who do not, and also to guide us in therapeutic techniques and strategies that would help a patient recover from a minimally conscious state.

9. Terri Schiavo deserves the opportunity to be treated for her minimally conscious state condition and she deserves to have the benefit of new technology that was not available prior to the court's original ruling on her condition.

I declare under the penalty of perjury under the laws of the State of Florida that the foregoing is true and correct.

Executed this 22 day of February 2005 in Jacksonville, Florida.

[signed by Jacob Green, M.D., Ph.D.], Declarant.

Declaration of James P. Kelly, M.D.

I, James P. Kelly, M.D., have personal knowledge of the facts stated in this declaration and, if called as a witness, I could and would testify competently thereto under oath. I declare as follows:

1. I am a licensed physician in Colorado and Illinois and an Attending Neurologist at the University of Colorado Hospital. I am a Diplomate in Neurology of the American Board of Psychiatry and Neurology and a Fellow of the American Academy of Neurology.

2. I am a Visiting Professor in the Department of Neurosurgery at the University of Colorado School of Medicine in Denver, Colorado.

3. I am an Examiner for the American Board of Psychiatry and Neurology.

4. I am currently Chairman of *AAN news* Subcommittee, Publications Committee of the American Academy of Neurology.

5. I serve on the Board of Governors for the International Brain Injury Association.

6. Since 2003, I have participated in Mild Traumatic Brain Injury and Mass Trauma Events for the National Center for Injury Prevention and Control, Centers for Disease Control and Prevention.

7. I was Director of the Brain Injury Program at the Rehabilitation Institute of Chicago from 1993 to 2000 and a member of the International Working Party on the Vegetative State

which was convened by the Royal Hospital for Neuro-Disability at the Royal College of Physicians in London, England in 1995.

8. Since 1994, I have been involved in a research project, "Assessment of the Minimally Conscious Patient," Development of an Evaluation Instrument for the Rehabilitation Institute of Chicago.

9. I am a co-author of the research that created the term "minimally conscious state" or "MCS" and directed the Aspen Neurobehavior Conferences in the 1990s where this new term was coined. MCS is intended to describe someone who is in a higher state of neurocognitive functioning than Vegetative State (VS). The term Minimally Conscious State (MCS) was not used in this context before the late 1990s.

10. I am a co-author on research papers coming out now, that have validated the Disorders of Consciousness Scale (DOCS), which was developed to distinguish between the states of coma, PVS, and MCS. Bedside tests, such as the DOCS, can be used to determine a person's level of consciousness.

11. A copy of my CV is attached for the reader's review.

12. Regarding Terri Schiavo, it would be inappropriate for me to offer a diagnosis or prognosis without examining her. However, the evidence presented in lay press accounts, radio broadcasts and internet sites indicating that she smiles appropriately, opens and closes her eyes on command and attempts to speak suggests that Terri Schiavo is not in a vegetative state but is in MCS (or possibly a higher level of functioning). If this is the case, Dr. Ron Cranford and other medical expert witnesses have been wrong in their statements that she is in a "persistent vegetative state." People in

vegetative state are consistently unconscious and do not interact in a meaningful way with people or the environment around them. There is only reflexive reaction or stereotyped response to external stimulation in VS.

13. I have been asked on three occasions to present the issues of the ethical dilemmas involved in Terri Schiavo's case to academic audiences, and I have reviewed the available information thoroughly for those occasions.

14. The issue of removing Ms. Schiavo's feeding tube is problematic as well. The actual physical removal of the tube is unnecessary and inappropriate. Feeding tubes should be left in place even if feedings are discontinued. The tube is the best route for medicines to be offered in "comfort care" protocols at the end-of-life. Removing the feeding tube and putting it back in place, as apparently has been done in Terri Schiavo's case, can be physically traumatic and painful. Regardless of the decision to stop or to continue feedings, there is no reason to consider removing the tube.

15. If an MRI of Terri Schiavo's brain has not been done in the last 12 months, one should be obtained to compare with earlier images to determine if her brain anatomy has undergone any changes over the interval of time. While it is possible that functional neuroimaging such as fMRI could offer information about the pattern of activation of her brain under specific stimulation applications, such testing is not routinely done for clinical purposes. This type of testing is considered experimental at this time and should be done only in academic settings with ongoing research protocols investigating coma/VS/MCS.

16. I would agree to review all pertinent medical records and examine Terri Schiavo to determine her level of consciousness, if

asked to do so by the court. Her swallowing would be best assessed by a skilled and experienced Speech Pathologist and a diagnostic Modified Barium Swallow radiological test.

I declare under the penalty of perjury under the laws of the State of Colorado that the foregoing is true and correct.

Executed this 7th day of March, 2005, in Denver, Colorado.

[signed by James P. Kelly, MD, FA AN], Declarant

Declaration of Peter J. Morin, M.D., Ph.d.

I, Peter J. Morin, have personal knowledge of the facts stated in this declaration and, if called as a witness, I could and would testify competently thereto under oath. I declare as follows:

1. I am a neurologist certified by the American Board of Psychiatry and Neurology. I practice neurology in Massachusetts and in Maine. I serve as Instructor of Neurology at the Boston University School of Medicine and Director of Outpatient Services for the New England GRECC (Geriatric Research Education and Clinical Center) at the Bedford VAMC. In that capacity, I supervise a 50-bed hospice ward for individuals in the advanced stages of dementia. I perform molecular research in neurology and neuroscience. I am also principal investigator for several neurological clinical research studies and serve as a neurologist for the Framingham Heart Study. I am providing this declaration as a neurologist, and not as a representative of Boston University or of the Department of Veterans Affairs.

2. My knowledge of Terri Schiavo's situation is indirect. I have not been provided an opportunity to review the medical record, nor to examine Ms. Schiavo. What knowledge I have about her situation derives from the news media and conversations with individuals who have followed the case carefully.

3. Based upon this information, I am concerned about the management of Ms. Schiavo's condition. As a neurologist who cares for the dying, I have a considerable interest in the rational management of such cases, both by attending physicians and by the court.

4. My first concern regards the quality of the information used by the court to establish Ms. Schiavo's intentions in the event of serious neurological injury. I have never met a 25-year-old outside of medical school who seriously considered such unusual possibilities regarding her mortality. In my experience, where an individual's wishes are uncertain (that is, where they have not previously been expressed in writing), the medical community defers to the more conservative course of action. This is especially true when there are family members who are willing and able to assume the burden of care. I am concerned that if patients' intentions are extrapolated from verbal reports, then physicians in general, and neurologists in particular, will be asked to terminate life support based upon less than definitive evidence of an individual's wishes. Surely the criteria for ending someone's life should be stringent and well-defined. Based upon what I know of Ms. Schiavo's situation, neither of these conditions has been met.

5. Secondly, I am concerned that the medical information under consideration is not contemporaneous with the decision at hand. It is my understanding that Ms. Schiavo has not had a medical, let alone a neurological, evaluation since 2002 or before. Since her neurological status is disputed, a decision should not be made based on outdated information. Given the uncertainty of her neurological status, current technology should be brought to bear on her current situation. It is my understanding that Ms. Schiavo had a neuroimaging test some three or more years ago and that her last electroencephalogram was more than ten years ago. Unless these tests were conclusive (i.e., showed indisputable, severe or extensive brain injury), they can hardly be considered relevant to her current neurological status. A quality and unbiased neurological evaluation and appropriate diagnostic tests need to be obtained at the time of

decision-making, even when the decision-making process has been prolonged. Failure to do so in a high-profile case such as this can only lower the threshold for inappropriately withholding lifesaving medical support for other neurologically compromised individuals.

6. I have discussed this matter with other neurologists. While all neurologists understand that some cases of coma and PVS are logically managed by not continuing life support, there is a general concern regarding management of highly uncertain cases. Even if it can be established that Ms. Schiavo's chances for a meaningful neurological recovery are very low, it cannot be established that her chances are zero. If there is no written indication that she would not wish to remain alive under these circumstances, and if there are family members willing to assume the burden of her care, then good neurological practice would give these family members the opportunity to provide that care. Established ethics societies and committees, some independent and some associated with national neurological organizations, should consider this matter and its implications prior to a final decision being rendered.

I declare under the penalty of perjury under the laws of the Commonwealth of Massachusetts that the foregoing is true and correct.

Executed this 8th day of March 2005, in Needham, Massachusetts.

[signed by Peter J. Morin, M.D., Ph.D], Declarant